SIDNEY REILLY

SIDNEY REILLY

The True Story of
The World's Greatest Spy

Michael Kettle

St. Martin's Press
New York

SIDNEY REILLY. Copyright © 1983 by Michael Kettle. All rights reserved.
Printed in the United States of America. No part of this book may be
used or reproduced in any manner whatsoever without written permission
except in the case of brief quotations embodied in critical articles or
reviews. For information, address St. Martin's Press, 175 Fifth Avenue,
New York, N.Y. 10010.

Library of Congress Cataloging in Publication Data
Kettle, Michael.
    Sidney Reilly: the true story of the world's greatest spy.

    1. Reilly, Sidney George, 1874–1925. 2. Spies—Great
Britain—Biography. 3. Spies—Soviet Union—Biography.
4. Soviet Union—History—Revolution, 1917–1921—Secret
service. 5. Counterrevolutions—Soviet Union. 6. Soviet
Union—History—Revolution, 1917–1921—Protest movements.
    I. Title.
UB271.G72R453 1984   327.1′2′0924 [B]   84-22852
ISBN 0-312-72338-5

First published in Great Britain by Transworld Publishers Ltd.
First U.S. Edition

10 9 8 7 6 5 4 3 2 1

For
Sue and John

AUTHOR'S NOTE

This book does not purport to be a full biography of Sidney Reilly – perhaps one cannot be written, as much went unrecorded, Reilly had a fascination for weaving false stories about himself (now it can be seen that it was mainly to protect his family); and much must be preserved in the archives of the Secret Intelligence Service, which are never made available.

Here, however, are some definite new facts about this fascinating man and his career; and it is hoped they will kill off some of the wilder speculation about him.

I am grateful to my literary agent, Michael Thomas, for his enthusiasm and encouragement with this project; and to my publisher, Patrick Janson-Smith, for achieving such an excellent production in so short a time.

I would also like to thank the Churchill Trustees (C and T Publications Limited) for their kind permission to reproduce two letters from Winston Churchill to Reilly, dated the 5th and 15th September 1924.

CONTENTS

SIDNEY REILLY

CHAPTER ONE

First Beginnings

Sidney Reilly was the most successful spy ever employed by the British Secret Service. At the height of his career between 1918 and 1924 he acted on a gigantic, heroic scale as a maker and indeed breaker of Governments. In 1918, he just failed to capture Lenin and Trotsky, and other members of the Bolshevik Central Committee, and overturn Russia's infant Bolshevik Government. But his attempt forced the Bolsheviks to unleash the Bolshevik Terror, which paved the way for the Russian Civil War proper, in which he played innumerable roles. In 1924, by means of a skilfully forged letter – allegedly from the Bolshevik leader Zinoviev to the British Communists, instructing them, among other things, to form Bolshevik cells in the British armed forces – he succeeded in bringing down Britain's new, and first ever, Labour Government. He had finally gone too far. He was ostracised by the British Secret Service and turned out into the cold, but for a year he ran a world-wide anti-Bolshevik Secret Service on his own. In 1925, the Bolsheviks lured him back to Soviet Russia, where he was captured by the Cheka, the Bolshevik Secret Police. While he was being interrogated, he tried to buy his life by revealing a few details of the British Secret Service and Foreign Office. His information was of immense use to the Bolsheviks in their infiltration of both Services, and their recruitment at the universities, especially at Trinity College, Cambridge, which Reilly had attended, and which, a few years later, was to nurture people like Burgess, Blunt and Michael Straight. 'There were a dozen students in the Trinity College (communist) cell when I joined it early in 1935,' records Michael Straight

11

in the *Observer* of 20 February 1983; it had evidently been going some little while.

These revelations did not, however, purchase Reilly's life. The Bolsheviks shot him.

Born as Sigmund Georgievich Rosenblum in 1874, he was the only son of Pauline and Grigory Jakovlevich Rosenblum, a rich Polish-Jewish landowner and contractor. His father owned an estate by the river Niemen near the bison forests in the Bielsk region of the Grodno *gubernia*, on land which was formerly part of the immense Wittgenstein properties. The estate was probably held in theory through a cover name, since although Jews in Russia and Russian Poland were permitted to own houses, they were not allowed to own landed property.

After the partition of Poland during the reign of Catherine II, a vast number of Jews had become Russian subjects; but their rights were severely restricted, as were their places of domicile. (Hence the Jewish 'Pale'). Exceptions were made for university graduates, merchants of the better sort (like the Rosenblums), and some artisans. Until then, Jews had no surname (they were simply known as 'son of'). Now, mainly for the purpose of military service, the Tsarist Police requested them to choose a name; most chose a German or Russian name as similar as possible to their Jewish names.

But the Jews were always under suspicion in Tsarist Russia. The universities in St Petersburg were only allowed to take 3% of Jewish students per year; in the provinces, this figure was 5%. Many intelligent Jewish boys were therefore educated abroad.

The Rosenblum family remember Sigmund's mother Pauline as a very beautiful woman, who knew the gifted pianist (and later Polish Prime Minister) Paderewski well. Sigmund's father Grigory was known as 'Hirsch' (which means 'stag' in German), and which, when russified, becomes 'Girsch', and hence 'Georgi' for short. In contrast to Pauline, Grigory is remembered as being '*rien d'extraordinaire*'. The Rosenblums were a prosperous family, very hospitable, and entertained a lot.

Sigmund's grandparents, Jacob and Henrietta Rosenblum, lived on the Mazowirtzka in Warsaw. In 1890, on their fiftieth wedding anniversary, an elaborate pictorial family tree was made up, with Sigmund, then sixteen, surrounded by his parents, and two sisters, for presentation to their grandparents. It still survives. His elder sister, no beauty, had a strongly hooked nose. She had a pathological fear of mice, married a doctor, and went to live near Voronezh. But she is fondly remembered as '*la bonne tante Marie*'. A member of the family states: 'We laughed at her, but we loved her.'

Sigmund's younger sister, Elena, was very beautiful, but committed suicide when only eighteen. The family presume she did so because of a love affair.

The 1890 photograph shows Sigmund as a boy with strong Jewish features, wavy but closely parted hair, and a determined expression.

Today, some of Sigmund's relatives hold positions of minor importance in the Soviet art world in Moscow; but I refrain from naming them. They would probably be surprised if they knew they were closely related to a famous spy.

But the clue to the mystery which Sigmund later used to encourage about his family background lies in the very difficult position of all Jewish people in Russian Poland, even more so than in Russia itself. His family was actively engaged in the Jewish emancipation movement, which led to the formation of the 'League for the Attainment of Complete Equality for Russian Jewry' in 1905; while a close relative, Leonty M. Bramson, was also a local deputy in the first Duma in 1906, when Reilly was just starting his own career. Later, the Bramson family became very well known in Jewish circles for charity work, and organising education amongst Jewish children.

*

13

Soon after the family picture was taken in 1890, Sigmund fell violently in love with his first cousin. The two families were horrified, and firmly forbade the match, which young Sigmund wished to make permanent. Already a rebellious youth, he abruptly left home, severing all connections with his family, and went abroad. This would have been when he attended university, if he did attend one at all; and later in life, when he wished particularly to impress anyone, he claimed that he had indeed attended Heidelberg University, studied philosophy, and obtained a PhD. (See, in particular, his letter of 10 October 1918 to the Dutch tug owner, Harry van den Bosch, who brought him out of Petrograd.) But Heidelberg denies all knowledge of him at any time, and under any of his assumed names. This important point has been double-checked: the West German Embassy in London approached the university on my behalf with the same question – and received the same answer.

It is not known for sure where he went; but the great home for Polish exiles at this time was the East End of London. The British police tolerated the clubs, some of which were Anarchist, that the Poles set up. Richard Deacon, in his *History of the British Secret Service* remarks that 'there were few English families who did not entertain as friend or visitor one of these unfortunate and suffering exiles'. The Rosenblums were well connected in Poland, and may well have had friends in London who looked after the young Sigmund and helped him bear with a life of relative poverty. In 1898, he married Margaret Thomas, a young widow with a little money. At the time he claimed to be a chemist. It was shortly after this that he joined the British Secret Intelligence Service, though no one knows how or why. The Russian Secret Police (the Okhrana) did not care for the large number of emigrés, violently hostile to the Tsar, in the East End; and Tsarist agents began a campaign of deliberately compromising some of the emigrés with the Metropolitan Police, with a view to their expulsion. Possibly he was such an emigré, and was recruited by the

14

SIS, who were anxious to enlist such refugees as British agents to keep a watch on the developing Russian oil industry and on Russian designs on India. This state of affairs occurred frequently in the 1890s. (See Richard Deacon, pp. 125–33.)

This event seems to have taken place about 1900. Shortly after, he changed his name to Reilly, (one of his father-in-law's christian names) and moved to the Far East. He lived in Port Arthur, the base of the Russian Far Eastern Fleet. The port had been forcibly conceded to Russia by China, a fact bitterly resented by Japan. Here he worked as partner in a firm of timber merchants called Grunberg and Reilly. Later, in the same city, he became manager of the Danish Compagnie Est-Asiatique. (See Geoffrey Bailey, *The Conspirators*, p. 21.) As the rivalry between Russia and Japan rapidly grew to boiling point, there seems little reason to doubt that he was there to report on this volatile situation to the SIS. But who paid for Reilly to go all the way to the Far East? It seems unlikely that the SIS would have financed him entirely; they may have been trying him out, leaving him to subsist on what he could earn, and on his wife's money. At all events, his reports seem to have been excellent. When the Russo-Japanese war broke out in 1904, he was back in London. He had passed his test with the SIS with flying colours, and they decided that they had a most promising recruit on their hands, who merited very special training.

In September 1904, under the name of Stanislaus George Reilly, he entered the Royal School of Mines in South Kensington to study electrical engineering. On his entry form, against the names of his parents, whose occupation is left blank, he wrote: 'I am independent of both.' He gave his address as 9, Powis Square, Bayswater. He further stated that he had: 'Indian experience in railway open-line work, constructiona and survey, in waterworks, buildings, roads, etc.' An official of the Royal School of Mines has written at the top of the form: 'Inspected Roorkee Coll. Cert. on which it is stated that S. G. Reilly was born on the 24th of April 1877.'

15

My research in the India Office records in London does indeed show that a certain Stanislaus George Reilly was born in Calcutta on that date; he was educated at a Catholic missionary school called St Fidelis at the hill station of Mussourie, graduated from Thomason Civil Engineering College at Roorkee University in 1897, and from 1899 to 1903, he was a railway engineer on small Indian railways. It was this alibi, carefully kept up to date all his life, which Reilly gave whenever the situation required it. Why he chose to be known as 'Stanislaus', another well-known Polish name, remains obscure.

Enquiries in India show this whole alibi to have been quite false. Roorkee University has no trace of him. Nor has the Bombay branch of the State Bank of India (formerly the Imperial Bank of India), where Reilly claimed to have banked for many years. Messrs Forbes Forbes Campbell and Company, for whom Reilly claimed to have worked as assistant manager from 1920–22, have no record of him as a former employee. Nor have the Bombay Water Board (of which Reilly claimed to have been the chief engineer from 1922–25) any trace of him in their records either. Yet in May 1925, just a few months before he disappeared, he joined the Institute of Civil Engineers in London, claiming to be the executive engineer on the construction of the Villa-puram-Trichinopoly branch of the South Indian railway; and no less than six people vouched for him (or rather perjured themselves). Later the same year, Reilly died at the hands of the Bolsheviks – yet he remained on the books of the Institute until 1948, when the SIS presumably made him 'resign'.

In July 1905, Reilly graduated from the Royal School of Mines with top marks (and was the only student not to study – in fact, not to need to study – a foreign language). He then went straight up to Trinity College, Cambridge, to do research into civil engineering. He is described in the College register as an advanced student, or pensioner. He lived out of College, presumably with his wife Margaret, at 8, Jesus Lane. His moral tutor was

16

a Mr Parry. Nothing is known of the results of his research. He gave his address on the College register as 63, Earls Court Square, London S.W. For his previous education, he wrote: 'Schools in India.' He gave his father's name as 'George'. His father, he added, was now dead. He claimed to have been born in Calcutta. He remained at Cambridge until 1907 or 1908, when he joined the Institute of Structural Engineers in London. Mr John A. Conway, a Fellow of the British Academy of Forensic Sciences, and an expert examiner of documents whose authenticity has been questioned, has at the author's request compared the handwriting on the entry forms for the Royal School of Mines and Trinity College with a later letter known to be by Reilly. Conway reported on 24 February 1970 that all three documents were in the same handwriting. He stated: 'I have compared the handwriting on the Royal School of Mines document with the Trinity College entry form, and because of the many similarities in writing quality, space, slope, letter proportions and letter designs, I am of the opinion that they are both in the same handwriting. I indicate the block form of capital 'S', the design of capital 'G', small 's' and 'y'. I have compared both with the letter of 25 September 1925 (Reilly's last letter, a photocopy of which was published by his last wife in 1931); and although there is a difference of some twenty years, I find between them strong similarities in the material features of letter proportions and letter designs. Although there are differences in slope, and in the completing of letter formations, I am of the opinion that the similarities indicate them to be in the same handwriting.'

Reilly was now a young, but highly-trained operative, fully equipped to report on Russia's oil and armaments industries. He had a carefully planned alibi to protect his family when he was in Russia. At first, however, he was sent to Persia, recently the subject of an entente between Britain and Russia, whereby that country was divided into British and Russian spheres of interest. He is credited – though there is no hard evidence to prove it – with having acquired the newly discovered Persian oilfields for the British from under the noses of the French.

He was then, as Bailey points out, definitely in St Petersburg, where he joined the armaments firm of Mandrokhovich and Chubersky. Russia was desperate to rearm after the calamity of the Russo-Japanese war, so business was good and commissions were excellent. He was soon on the way to amassing a small fortune. He was also engaged as the Russian agent for the German firm of Blohm and Voss of Hamburg, who were reconstructing the Russian Fleet, severely mauled by Japan; and he was able to send the latest German naval designs to the Admiralty in London, and increase his income from commissions still further. Rarely has a spy been able to carry out his legitimate duties with such personal profit.

Reilly was soon mixing with important people in Tsarist circles, for, in Deacon's words, he was a 'charmer, gregarious, an excellent mixer at all levels, with a reputation as a man who could arrange complex cosmopolitan business deals, and a gay Lothario who loved parties. All who knew him spoke of his magnetic personality, and his supreme gift of coaxing people to do things for him. He disarmed suspicion by behaving in a roisteringly extrovert manner, even deliberately courting attention.' He began to collect Napoleonic relics, and soon had a luxurious flat. According to his last wife, who perhaps exaggerated, the flat contained 'quite a museum of objects of Renaissance art, and his library of the finest editions extended to more than three thousand volumes. He drove the smartest equipages, and had as fine horses as were to be found anywhere in Russia. Calm, dignified, immaculate, wherever he went . . .'

This deliberate courting of attention was all part of the act. He indeed enjoyed high life and was a great womaniser; but, underneath it all, as his professional reports make clear, he was a very shrewd man. Part

18

thug, part chameleon, he was above all a skilled and ruthless manipulator of other people. He used women as easily as men, even in the most desperate of revolutionary conspiracies. There is no instance of any woman ever giving him away – some even went to their deaths in the terrible summer of 1918 rather than betray him.

He remained faithful to one woman all his life – his cousin, by now a widow with two young children in Warsaw. She had had an unhappy marriage to a wealthy businessman called Neufeldt, a sick man who had eventually died insane. Each time Reilly travelled to London, he stopped off at Warsaw to see her. She alone of all his family knew what he was really doing. From St Petersburg in March 1913, he sent her a Leipzig edition of the Rubaiyat of Omar Khayyam in German. It was bound in beautiful green leather, with a gold fan on the front of the book. Inside, Reilly had inscribed the German translation of the twenty-ninth stanza:

> *'Into this universe, and why not knowing,*
> *Nor whence, like water willy-nilly flowing,*
> *And out of it, as wind along the waste,*
> *I know not whither, willy-nilly blowing.'*

But when he chanced to meet any of his family in St Petersburg, he ignored them. Once, before the war, he found himself sitting next to one of his cousins, in the shaving saloon of a fashionable club called Maullé's. When the cousin tried to speak to him, Reilly cut him dead, although many years later in London, he was to apologise for this.

All this while, from 1908 to the beginning of the Great War, some official in Delhi carefully compiled Reilly's alibi as an Anglo-Indian railway engineer. By 1914, he had become manager and chief engineer of the Dehri-Rolitas light railway.

On the outbreak of war, Reilly was a wealthy man with a secure position in St Petersburg high society. He had a beautiful Russian wife called Nadine, who had divorced her husband – an official in the Russian Ministry of Marine – to marry him. (Margaret had been sent packing back to England – she evidently did not fit in with Reilly's new life – and his recent marriage was bigamous). Reilly and Nadine now moved to Japan, a member of the Allied Entente, whose support was limited to the supply of munitions. Reilly, acting for the Russo-Asiatic Bank, became the chief commission agent for the purchase of Japanese supplies for the Russian Army – a highly lucrative post. They do not appear to have remained long in Japan, soon moving to New York to organise the purchase and transmission of American supplies. Reilly had his office at 120 Broadway.

According to Bailey, he gave up this task in 1916. Leaving Nadine in New York, he moved to Canada where he enlisted in the Royal Flying Corps. Shortly afterwards, he was in London, where he was taken up by the Admiralty – he had made his mark there many years before by supplying them with German naval designs destined for the Russian Fleet. For the next two years, again according to Bailey, he was engaged in secret missions to Germany, either obtaining naval information or sabotaging ships. It is understood that he gave complete satisfaction to his new masters.

In the spring of 1918, Reilly's career took yet another dramatic change of direction. Russia was by now out of the war and in the hands of the Bolsheviks. The British War Cabinet was uncertain how to deal with the problem. Lloyd George, the Prime Minister, decided to send a man with special qualifications to explore the Russian situation.

CHAPTER TWO

The Baltic Fleet

Since the Bolshevik revolution of November 1917, the British, knowing that a huge German offensive was to be launched on the Western Front in the spring, had been playing a double game with the Russians. On the one hand, Lloyd George had personally sent out Robert Bruce Lockhart, the former British Consul in Moscow, as political agent to the Bolsheviks; on the other hand, the War Cabinet had definitely decided in early February 1918 against granting even *de facto* recognition to the infant Bolshevik Government. They were prepared to recognise other groups in the former Russian Empire, however, and had promised large sums of money to the anti-Bolshevik groups near the Don if they would fight on against Germany. But no money had got through, even though the War Cabinet had authorised the purchase of most of the Russian banks, which in turn controlled most of the Russian economy.

The War Cabinet had also, since late January, been pressing for Allied intervention in Russia to prevent the Germans from seizing Russian resources. The key to intervention lay with Japan. The Allies were by now acutely short of manpower. American troops were coming, but exactly when still had to be worked out. Japan, alone of the Allies, had a large army, but she declined to use it far beyond her own borders, and thus on no existing Allied front. She would, and could, however, use it in Eastern Russia; but it was rightly felt that her main concern was to seize part of the Russian eastern maritime provinces for herself. As there was strong latent rivalry between Japan and the United States in the Far East, Japan cautiously refused to move, even into the port of Vladivostok, without American consent. The Allies, especially the British, had put their first proposal for Japan to intervene to Washington on 24 January, but President Wilson would not be moved. They had renewed their request on 25 February, just as the Bolsheviks were taking Russia out of the war. All through March and April, the President continued to withhold his consent.

In London, the great German offensive on the Western Front of 21 March had produced a hectic atmosphere which bordered on panic. Bruce Lockhart was adamant, in his wires from Moscow, that if only Japan could be restrained the Bolsheviks would themselves renew the war with Germany. On 15 April, he had wired the terms on which Trotsky might agree to invite the Allies to intervene against the Germans. But this crossed with an ultimatum from the Foreign Secretary Balfour to Trotsky that, unless matters were agreed within fourteen days, the British would radically reconsider such policy as they had towards the Bolsheviks. Balfour had heard that there was to be an anti-Bolshevik coup on 1 May – which in the event turned out to be a complete fiasco. Lockhart's influence in London had in any case declined. The War Cabinet was now faced with a general impasse in its Russian policy.

As things got more desperate on the Western Front, Lloyd George effectively jettisoned Lockhart, whom he himself had sent out in opposition to some of the War Cabinet. There is evidence from what Reilly himself said in early May that Lloyd George, around this time, asked 'C' if he had a really good man to send out to Russia. 'C' – Captain Mansfield Cumming, a former naval officer now at the head of SIS – brought Reilly along to Downing Street for a talk with Lloyd George. The Prime Minister explained the position. He was dissatisfied with Lockhart's reports. He wanted firm news of real Bolshevik intentions at once. The Bolsheviks were causing everyone a great deal of trouble, just as affairs were becoming more critical by the hour in France. If things got worse, Lloyd George hinted, it might be no bad thing if the Bolsheviks went under. He undoubtedly made such a suggestion obliquely, so as not to compromise himself; but he was a past-master at such things. Reilly would have got the message.

It may well have been the Admiralty that persuaded 'C' to take Reilly to Lloyd George in the first place. For the Admiralty itself had strong reasons for wanting Reilly back in Russia. Not only had he done good work for them over the past two years; but, far more important, he had been closely involved in the reconstruction of the Russian warships after the Russo-Japanese war. The Admiralty was seriously concerned about the Baltic Fleet, which the Germans, now in Helsinki, might seize. The Admiralty reckoned that the Baltic Fleet still consisted of 5 battleships, 9 cruisers, seventy destroyers and twenty-six submarines. This was undoubtedly a considerable over-estimate, and must have included old ships, ships temporarily out of commission, and ships being built. But the First Lord was particularly anxious about the destroyers: the British Grand Fleet was somewhat short of this class of warship; and if any of these Russian destroyers fell into German hands, the naval situation would become 'very serious'. The Admiralty had instructed Captain Francis Cromie, the British Naval Attaché in Petrograd (as St Petersburg was now called), to prepare a plan for their destruction. But it was felt that Cromie was politically too inexperienced to carry it out. He needed an assistant, and there was no one who knew more of this particular type of 'politics' than Reilly. He had helped rebuild the Baltic Fleet; he was the obvious man to help blow it up.

Reilly's despatch to Russia was approved. Posing as a Bolshevik emigré, he went to Maxim Litvinov, the unofficial Bolshevik delegate in England, and obtained a pass to return to Russia.

Reilly, it seems, returned to Russia in late April 1918 via Murmansk and Petrograd, just as President Wilson was

23

turning down the latest British proposal for Japan to intervene in Eastern Russia. He first tried a direct approach. In the uniform of a British lieutenant, he marched up to the Kremlin on 7 May, and demanded to see Lenin. He must have produced some credentials, as he was ushered straight in to see one of Lenin's close colleagues. He had been sent out especially by Lloyd George, said Reilly, to obtain first-hand information on real Bolshevik aims, as the British Government was dissatisfied with Lockhart's reports (so the Assistant Commissar for Foreign Affairs that evening told Lockhart, who records that he 'knew instinctively' that his informant was speaking the truth). But Reilly was rebuffed.

'There was an air of desolation over Moscow,' records a British officer who was there at this time. 'Few of the shops were open, and those that were open were almost empty. The famous store of Muir and Merrilees had nothing in it. There were no droshkies in the place, for all the horses had been eaten, or had died of starvation. Ordinary life was at a standstill.'

Reilly then had to leave urgently for Petrograd. The former Russian capital was in an even worse state than Moscow. Dead horses lay strewn along the unkempt streets, now totally deserted save for the endless bread queues – and the Cheka and its agents were everywhere. Such were the combined effects of the Bolshevik revolution and three years of exhausting warfare. Reilly's return was urgent, for Captain Cromie had just completed a scheme to block Kronstadt harbour and blow up four battleships and fourteen destroyers (the only ships reckoned to be in active service), at a total cost of some £300,000.

This proposal caused extreme dissension when it was brought before the War Cabinet in London. It was argued that to take such action might well turn all Russians, not only the Bolsheviks, completely against the British, and thus propel them into German arms – which the War Cabinet wanted above all to prevent. It

24

could not possibly be pretended that the British had not been involved. Argument raged back and forth. In the end, the Prime Minister decided that there must be a special discussion on Russian policy before any decision was taken on blowing up the Baltic Fleet; meanwhile, Cromie had authority to set his plan in action only if the Germans were about to seize the ships.

At the special session of the War Cabinet on 11 May, it was decided to hold Cromie's plan in reserve, to press Trotsky himself to blow up the Baltic Fleet, and to allow part of the Czech Legion to turn about, and go up to North Russia to defend the area against the Germans. (The Czech Legion, two divisions strong, consisted of Czechs who had been living in Russia before the war, together with deserters from the Austrian Army. This body of men had kept their cohesion, good morale and arms, amidst the chaos of the Russian Revolution, and now wished to leave Russia to found a democratic Czechoslovak state. At this time, they were strung out in trains along the Siberian railway; and as they trundled through Russia and Siberia to find ships, they hoped, in the Far East, they had clashed with the Bolsheviks over the question of retaining their arms.)

The War Cabinet also agreed to send a nucleus of Allied troops to Russia to help Trotsky repel any further German incursions; if Japan and America then saw what was happening, they could hardly hold back. It was decided, in fact, to force President Wilson's hand. The Allies, it was agreed, must now be prepared to act without waiting for a Bolshevik invitation. It was further decided to send a small British force to North Russia to act as a rallying point for any Russian or other troops in the area, and to train the Czechs.

The matter was then put to Washington. President Wilson was agreeable to intervention in North Russia, though not in Siberia. The Foreign Office then wired to Lockhart to ask Trotsky about the Czechs. The Russian leader agreed to permit part of the Czech Legion to go to

North Russia. The Admiralty also wired the Cabinet decisions to Cromie. He was told to extend his operations to ships under construction; and Lockhart was instructed to acquire the extra finance which Cromie would need. Again, Trotsky agreed to co-operate. Thus, British and Bolshevik plans for the destruction of the Baltic Fleet went along, more or less hand in hand.

Cromie wired back that sentiment within the Baltic Fleet was becoming strongly anti-Bolshevik, for the whole Fleet was being told, by means of well-placed rumour, that Trotsky had already agreed with the Germans either to hand over or to blow up the warships. The crucial destroyers, he added, were being sent up to Lake Ladoga, as a further protection against German seizure. What part Reilly played in all this is unclear, but he was undoubtedly involved. Cromie, the Cabinet had been told, was being assisted 'by well-known Secret Service officers.'

In mid-May, Lenin made an important move. Seeing both Allies and Germans encroaching more and more on Bolshevik Russia, Lenin made it plain that the Allies would not be invited to intervene, and proposed to the Germans to settle outstanding difficulties by means of trade talks in Berlin. At the same time, though the Germans continued their financial support for the Bolsheviks, they opened secret talks with the Don Cossacks and Monarchist groups, in case the Bolsheviks fell from power.

On 16 May, Cromie reported that his preparations would be completed in two days; he intended to act on the 21 or 22 May, as the Germans were exepcted to enter Petrograd on the 23 May. This crucial wire was delayed in transmission; for on 23 May, as a British force arrived at Murmansk, Cromie wired again that rumours of German occupation of Petrograd had receded, and he had not taken any action. But the scheme was now completed, and could not be delayed for more than a month, owing to his agents' poor morale.

But all these carefully-laid British plans for Russia

then went wrong. Cromie wired again that as rumours of German occupation of Petrograd receded, his agents had begun to talk about what they were going to do, 'a fatal Russian fault'. This soon reached Trotsky's ears. He had unwittingly become a British tool. He decided on drastic action against the British. On 25 May, he had the Commander of the Baltic Fleet arrested as a counter-revolutionary agent, and ordered all local Soviets in Russia and Siberia to disarm or shoot any armed Czech they found. The Czechs refused to disarm, or allow part of the Legion to go to North Russia. They launched a revolt against the Bolsheviks, and pitched battles took place all along the Siberian railway, which was soon more or less in Czech hands.

In late May, as German attacks continued relentlessly on the Western Front, British frustration over Russia increased. At an Anglo-French conference in London (long before news of the Czech revolt had reached the Allied capitals) the French formally forbade the British to initiate Allied intervention in order to force President Wilson's hand. Once again the British were at an impasse over Russian policy.

CHAPTER THREE

The Lettish Conspiracy

While in Petrograd, Reilly assumed the alias of a Monsieur Massino (in fact, the former surname of his wife Nadine), calling himself a Turkish and Oriental merchant. In the spring of 1918 (presumably while on duty with Cromie over the Baltic Fleet), he could often be seen about the more elegant and expensive cafes of Petrograd, which were still open. Well-groomed, wealthy-looking, with a high, sloping forehead, smouldering eyes and sensuous lips, he seemed on equally good terms with the new regime as he was with the survivors of the old, so Bailey tells us.

In late May, with 'the pro-British Czechs actively intervening against the Bolsheviks, the time had come for Reilly to turn his attention away from the Baltic Fleet, which the Germans were now unlikely to seize since they were engaged in talks with the Bolsheviks in Berlin. The time had come for action against the Bolsheviks themselves.

In Moscow, Reilly got in touch, through old acquaintances, with many ex-Tsarist officers who were in hiding. The policy of the Bolsheviks towards these out-of-work Russian officers was highly ambivalent. Some were desperately needed to act as 'military specialists' with the new Red Army; but most were distrusted. If there was the slightest sign that they would not prove loyal to the new regime, the Bolsheviks arrested them. Some were blackmailed, by having their families seized as hostages. These officers were Reilly's potential recruits. Soon he had set up an extensive network of agents among them. He was known as 'Mr Constantine', a Greek merchant. At the house of one of his best agents, a ballerina called

Dagmara K. of the Moscow Arts Theatre, he met a Miss Friede, whose brother was a Colonel in the Lettish Rifles. Colonel Friede was the Bolshevik Chief of Staff in Moscow, but he hated his new masters. He was soon passing on Bolshevik military plans and orders to Reilly, who somehow got them through to London. With Colonel Friede's help, Reilly also managed to obtain a pass as Commissar 'Relinsky' in the Cheka, which was to prove invaluable.

Now Friede was a Latvian. Reilly quickly realised that, while Trotsky was feverishly trying to form a new Red Army, the Bolsheviks still in fact had to rely on three small forces: the original Red Guards, mainly factory workers and sailors, whose revolutionary zeal far outran their military capabilities; a few thousand Chinese, who had been used to construct the Murmansk railway, and would cut anyone's throat for food; and the Latvian regiments, who retained their cohesion, like the Czechs, and had been more or less bought by the Bolsheviks, and acted as a Praetorian Guard. The Latvians were far more capable than the Red Guards and the Chinese, and loathed the Germans who had over-run their country. Reilly saw that these mercenaries could be bribed to turn against their present masters in Moscow, whereupon the numerous Russian officers – if only they could unite – could easily take over, and then reopen the war against Germany.

On 7 June, as the Bolshevik delegation – officially a trade delegation – arrived in Berlin, the British decided to keep in step, and send a British trade delegation to Moscow.

On 13 June, *The Times* printed the first news, from a German source, that the departing Czechs were in disagreement with the Bolsheviks, and that Trotsky had ordered the local Soviets to disarm them. Two days later, *The Times* carried news of the Czech revolt: several thousand Czechs had managed to get through to the port of Vladivostok. This caused great excitement in all the Allied capitals. President Wilson now thought he could see the outline of a plan which would satisfy the constant badgering of his Allied colleagues for full-scale intervention in the Far East. But it was to be another three crucial weeks before he made up his mind.

The Czech revolt continued with growing help from various groups of Russian officers. Finally, on 6 July, President Wilson agreed to a small force of Americans and Japanese – 14,000 from each country – to intervene in the Far East to save the Czechs from being slaughtered by the Bolsheviks. The race was now on.

In Moscow, where everyone was expecting Allied intervention at any moment, this coincided with a political and military revolt against the Bolsheviks. The political revolt was launched by the left-wing of the great Social Revolutionary party (known as the left SRs). They had been in loose alliance with the Bolsheviks ever since the Bolshevik revolution, but had only agreed to the humiliating treaty of Brest-Litovsk in March with great misgivings. The left SRs were particularly strong in the Ukraine, where the Germans were behaving with great barbarity against the local peasantry to obtain the necessary grain supplies. The left SRs were violently anti-German. They knew that the Bolsheviks were still receiving German subsidies, and in some cases were still practically carrying out orders from the German Embassy in Moscow; but they did not know that Lenin had sent a Bolshevik delegation to Berlin. The left SRs were adamant that war should again be declared against the Germans in the Ukraine. The Bolsheviks naturally refused. Lenin was determined both to end this dependence on Germany and to eliminate the left SRs at a stroke.

On 4 July, the Fifth Congress of Soviets met in the Bolshoi Theatre to resolve their differences. The left SRs were defeated, and accused the Bolsheviks of being the lackeys of Berlin. Two days later (6 July), the former terrorist Boris Savinkov, with his group of Russian officers, seized several towns around Moscow, though they later lost control of all but Jaroslavl, to the north-east of the capital. At the same time, a member of the Cheka (with Lenin's secret approval) called at the German Embassy, and assassinated the German Ambassador. At this, the left SRs launched an ill-prepared revolt in Moscow itself. Lenin blamed the killing of the German Ambassador on the British and the French; he claimed it was designed as provocation to get Russia to declare war on Germany again. The left SR uprising was easily put down; the party was eliminated from the Government; and the Bolsheviks could turn their full attention to Savinkov's revolt. Savinkov desperately hoped that he could hold on long enough for the Allies to intervene; but Allied affairs, even after President Wilson's decision, were still moving with desperate slowness.

What links were there, if any, between the left SRs and Savinkov? And were they through British agents? It is certain that the left SRs, Savinkov and Bolsheviks all had agents within each others' organisations. Captain George Hill (another SIS man) was at this time organising guerrilla action against the Germans in the Ukraine, and was certainly in touch with the left SRs, as well as Savinkov, whom he did not like. 'My distrust of him was a matter of frequent contention between myself and Sidney Reilly, who had a blind belief in the man,' Hill later recorded. But if the link was Reilly, it certainly went wrong. On the afternoon of 6 July, while Lockhart was waiting at the Bolshoi Theatre for the Soviet Congress to resume, unaware that the German Ambassador had been assassinated, Reilly suddenly burst into his box, pale and agitated, with 'only the vaguest idea of what had occurred'. He only knew that 'something had gone wrong.' Reilly whispered that the killing of the German Ambassador (thinking it to be the work of the left SRs, who were much given to political assassination) was meant to be the signal for a general uprising against the Bolsheviks. But the left SRs, fooled by rumours of an imminent Allied landing at Archangel, had acted too hastily; they had seized the Post Office, but the Bolshoi Theatre was now ringed by loyal Lettish Rifles. When a

31

nervous sentry dropped a hand grenade, causing a loud explosion on the floor above, Reilly and a French agent began to empty their pockets, tearing up such documents as they had on them, and eating those which it was too dangerous to stuff between the cushions of the sofa.

Reilly was clearly unprepared for the events of 6 July, which suggests that his intelligence network was still neither as efficient nor as far-flung as he might have wished.

In Berlin, nothing was done about the murder of the German Ambassador. Lenin's explanation was accepted. The Kaiser decided that they must continue to support the Bolsheviks, because that still suited German interests best.

But the German Embassy in Moscow now thought the end of the Bolshevik regime was at hand. The Embassy reported to Berlin that the leaders of the Latvian regiments had been in touch with them, even after taking a major share in putting down the left SR revolt in Moscow, because they too believed the Bolshevik Government was about to fall. They wanted the German Government to allow them to return home in freedom; they also asked for an amnesty. On 10 July, the German Embassy forwarded this request to the Foreign Ministry in Berlin, which granted the amnesty. Reilly would have to act swiftly if he wished to out-bid the Germans and gain the services of the Latvians for the Allies.

The survival of the Bolsheviks depended entirely on them. On 28 July, the German Military Attaché in Moscow reported that the Latvian troops numbered 30,000. If the German High Command did decide on military action to bring about a change of Russian regime, they would need only one efficient battalion, provided the Latvians were first neutralised; this could be achieved by bribes. But if the Latvians were hostile, the Germans would need to commit six divisions to a costly new campaign on the Eastern Front.

On 1 August, Allied troops finally landed at Archangel, after a well-prepared coup in the town against

32

the local Bolsheviks. Their arrival, however, came too late to save Savinkov, whose revolt had been suppressed. In Moscow, the Bolshevik Government panicked. Next day, the Bolshevik Foreign Commissar went in person to the German Embassy to ask for German military support against the British to North Russia (something which the Germans had long pressed on the Bolsheviks, which the latter had, up to now, sedulously refused). The Foreign Commissar stressed that an open German-Bolshevik military alliance was still impossible, and that German troops must be kept out of Petrograd. They also asked the Germans to stop supporting the Don Cossacks in South Russia.

The new German Ambassador reported to the Foreign Ministry in Berlin that this *démarche* showed the 'extremes of the dilemma' in which the Bolsheviks now found themselves. He urged the German Government to pretend to fall in with this Bolshevik request for intervention, but at the last moment to make a common front with the Cossack leaders, and overthrow the Bolsheviks. Since this advice was quite contrary to Foreign Ministry directives, the German Foreign Minister ordered his Ambassador to leave Moscow forthwith, and report to Berlin. The German Embassy in Moscow was now practically closed.

In the old British Embassy in Petrograd, Reilly now took the politically inexperienced Cromie in hand. Together they had assembled between £840,000 and £1 million sterling for the sabotage of the Baltic Fleet. Now this money could be used for preparing a coup, so that Allied troops could have as bloodless an entry into Petrograd as they had had into Archangel. The Bolsheviks realised this all too well, and were determined to get hold of this sterling hoard first, using any methods. Something of the struggle can be seen in a telegram sent by Cromie on 5 August. During the last two days, he began, the British and French consulates had been raided, and about 7,000 Russian officers and civilians had been arrested, the majority of them being sent to

Kronstadt. The arrests were still proceeding, and whole-sale assassination was probable. 'We have sent a memorandum to Lockhart (in Moscow),' Cromie went on, 'suggesting an ultimatum be sent in to the (Bolshevik) Government that if any harm falls on the (Russian) officers, the (Allied) Expeditionary Force will take the form of a punitive expedition.' (Many of these officers were Cromie's personal friends.) 'Suggest a proclamation be issued stating if these officers are shot, the (Bolshevik) Government will be held strictly responsible. This would bring very large section of public over to our side.'

Cromie then went on to relate a remarkable offer they had just had. The Bolshevik Government, he reported, had asked for £1 million sterling. Cromie and Reilly had replied that they were prepared to advance it on the following conditions:

1) At an exchange rate of 50 roubles to the £, and delivery at Archangel (the current exchange rate being 40);
2) Guarantees for the safety of all foreigners in Petrograd and Moscow; and
3) Guarantees for the safety of all Russian officers arrested.

Negotiations had not yet started, Cromie went on. He asked for more information about future Allied plans. They had had several offers of river gunboats, etc, but had refused such offers until they were sure they could be sent, and that fuel would be available. Cromie concluded: 'Great discontent here in Red Army chiefly Let (i.e. Lettish), amongst whom we are agitating. Bolsheviks (in) general very nervous.'

Transmission of this last paragraph in the normal naval code was undoubtedly most unwise, and probably made Cromie, if this wire was intercepted (and there is fair reason to suppose that it was), a marked man. To admit to tampering with the loyalty of the Lettish troops at such a desperate moment would make Cromie *per-*

34

sona non grata, to say the least – and these were not normal times. It is impossible to say whether the alleged Bolshevik demand of £1 million sterling in return for sparing the lives of the arrested men was in any way genuine. If it was genuine, the Bolsheviks very soon dropped it.

In his next wire direct to General Poole (the Allied Commander at Archangel), Cromie reported that all Allied officers were now forbidden to send wires abroad or within Russia, or move from one town to another. During the past two days, British subjects had been arrested by the Bolsheviks without any charge being made against them; but only two had been detained. Cromie was protesting vigorously, and expected an explanation the next day. 'If unsatisfactory,' he warned Poole, 'propose informing Soviet that as British officials and subjects are threatened with arrest, and possibly bodily harm, we have informed our Government and have requested every effort be made by our troops (at Archangel) to advance to our rescue.' All British officials, who were arrested at Moscow on 5 August, had now been released, and were under house arrest. They had sent a warning that they would probably be evacuated, and that the British community in Petrograd should be ready to leave with them.

Cromie went on to warn Poole: 'Commissar here (Uritsky) threatens to intern all Allied subjects as soon as you occupy Vologda.' (This town was halfway between Archangel and Petrograd). Cromie had destroyed all cyphers but the present one, and repeated that he was not allowed to wire in any direction; Poole was thus asked to inform the Admiralty of this message. 'Position of Soviet power in Petrograd is becoming rapidly untenable,' Cromie went on. 'They are giving orders for evacuation of various units and places. It is evident they are in touch with Germans,' he stated. 'Lenin is at Peterhof and a Yacht under Swedish flag (is) ready to take him away.' (This latter statement was not however true.)

35

In Moscow, Bruce Lockhart, who was about to leave Russia anyhow, hastily began to collect financial support for the White Russians at the – still unraided – American Consulate in Moscow, where the Allied Consuls were now holding surreptitious daily meetings.

Then it suddenly became known that the Allied force which had landed at Archangel numbered only 1,200 troops! Bolshevik relief was all too evident. The Allies had brought such a small number because a large contingent of Czech troops was expected in North Russia. The decision of the Czech Legion not to split up had never reached London.

In Petrograd, Reilly was desperately trying to find out exactly what the Bolsheviks were plotting with the Germans. About 14 August, matters became clear. Ludendorff dropped his military objections to the German-Bolshevik trade treaty; and this was rapidly reflected in the editorials of the Berlin newspapers. As it became known that the Bolshevik delegates, who were back in Moscow, were returning to Berlin to sign the treaty, the Bolshevik mission in Berlin wired to Moscow that the Germans had now agreed to send troops, via Petrograd and Vologda, to the North Russian front, under the nominal command of Russian officers.

Reilly had access to what was passing on the wires between Moscow and Berlin, and his plan was now complete. The Latvians were to arrest Lenin and Trotsky and, after distributing leaflets with details of the trade treaty in Moscow, smother them with ridicule by parading them through the streets (clad, apparently, only in their shirts). The Russian officers would then be mobilised, and a Provisional Military Government set up, which would recall the Constituent Assembly. Part of the newly assembled Russian force would march to join the Czechs on the Volga, while part would march to Petrograd, where a rising would take place. Uritsky (head of the Petrograd Cheka, and generally in charge of the old Russian capital) would be arrested; and the bridges in Petrograd, and on the Petrograd–Vologda railway, would be blown up to stop German troops getting through to Archangel. The signal for the coup would be news of the actual signature of the trade treaty in Berlin.

By now, the Bolsheviks at least knew that Allied officials and secret agents knew more than they should of Bolshevik plans, even if they did not know the details of the coming Allied coup. On 15 August, when the Danish Minister (who was looking after British interests) went to see Uritsky about the release of British and French hostages, Uritsky stated flatly that he knew what was going on in the old British Embassy. Acting strictly according to precedent, the Bolsheviks decided to use agents-provocateurs to spring the plot before it was ready. Cromie indeed, at this moment, seems to have abandoned security. He sent a note to Lockhart, via a youth called Smidchen who appears to have been an agent-provocateur. In it, Cromie confirmed that he was making his own way out of Russia, and said that he hoped to leave with a bang; Smidchen, he added, might be of some use. Smidchen took the note straight to Colonel Berzin, a Latvian, who passed it on to Peters (deputy head of the Cheka), also a Latvian, who had a wife in England.

The Bolshevik position was desperate. The Latvians themselves were now under suspicion, on the Volga and elsewhere. Colonel Berzin, seemingly disillusioned with the Bolsheviks, had had to break off negotiations with the Germans when the Embassy was recalled to Berlin. Berzin was now in touch with Colonel de Vertement (head of the French Deuxième Bureau in Moscow), and with Xenophon Kalamatiano (of the American Secret Service). Reilly had made discreet contact with Berzin through his colleague Captain Hill. Whether Berzin's change of heart was in any way genuine is unclear. But the Allies now had four columns – of sorts – outside the city, and their fifth column inside. It was evident that something was going to happen. Berzin and his colleagues decided to go to Lockhart and obtain a pass through the lines. If the Bolsheviks went under, even loyal Latvian comrades had a right to save themselves. If the Bolsheviks survived, they could denounce Lockhart for taking part in a plot, and become Bolshevik heroes.

On 15 August, therefore, Colonel Berzin, armed with Cromie's note and with Smidchen in tow, called on Lockhart at his flat in Moscow. The Latvians, he said, were ready to go over to the British on the Archangel front. Could Lockhart give them a pass? After conferring with his French colleague, Lockhart duly did so the next day, and put Berzin in touch with Reilly. These two met on 17 August, and discussed the despatch of Bolshevik units to Vologda, which would be handed over to the British, and the seizure of Lenin and Trotsky at a Central Committee meeting in Moscow. Reilly evidently gave Berzin a considerable amount of roubles. The following day, Reilly told Lockhart that his negotiations with the Latvians were going well. After Lockhart had left Moscow, he added, he might perhaps be able to use them to stage a coup in Moscow. Lockhart, who perhaps did not wish to know, claims that he and the French told Reilly that he was not to do so. *But*, it should be noted that entries in Bruce Lockhart's diary between 11 August and 31 August, which, it is clear from a summary, contain details of his relations with Reilly at this crucial period, have been withheld; these will not be available to researchers until the end of the century. Whatever Lockhart actually said, Reilly decided to go ahead.

It will be recalled that Reilly had for some time been in touch with Colonel Friede (the Bolshevik Chief of Staff in Moscow, also a Latvian), who had been passing on military information to Reilly. On 20 August, Colonel Friede's sister told Reilly that the Central Committee would meet in the Bolshoi Theatre on the 28 August. Would this be too soon? Would the trade treaty be signed by then? Reilly had further meetings with Berzin to discuss the seizure of certain Bolshevik offices to obtain details of the trade treaty.

38

Reilly was now being urged to meet his Allied colleagues to arrange for co-operation. In Berlin, there were several minor, last minute hitches to the treaty; but on 23 August the Bolshevik delegates agreed to sign it. This news was no doubt rapidly passed to Moscow. That day or the next, Reilly attended a meeting at the American Consulate – much against his will – where he found the American Consul Poole, the French Consul Grenard, Colonel de Vertement – and Réné Marchand (the Moscow correspondent of the newspaper *Figaro*). Marchand surprised Reilly by suddenly asking him for his name. Reilly muttered 'Rice', and went off with Colonel de Vertement into another room. While they were in animated discussion, Reilly suddenly noticed that Marchand had come into the room and was listening.

Moscow and other Russian towns were on the verge of starvation. On 25th August, *Izvestia* reported that Allied agents had just blown up three precious food trains at Voronezh station, as the Don Cossacks, with German backing, broke into Voronezh province. Marchand, who had in fact only overheard part of the conversation between Reilly and the French Colonel, went straight to the Bolsheviks, and told them that he had just heard this man 'Rice' and Colonel de Vertement discussing plans for the demolition of bridges on the Petrograd-Vologda railway (along which German troops were to proceed, en route for the Archangel front). The Bolsheviks listened attentively to Marchand: more evidence, they told him, of the wicked imperialists trying to starve out the people of Petrograd. But they must have been alarmed. How much did Reilly and Colonel de Vertement know? It was announced that the Central Committee meeting had been delayed until 6 September.

The trade treaty was finally signed in Berlin on 27 August, by which the Bolsheviks agreed to sell part of the Baku oil to the Germans, connive at German use of the Black Sea Fleet, and pay a very large indemnity. In return, the Germans agreed to withdraw their support

39

from the Don Cossacks, to permit Bolshevik trade in grain and coal with the Ukraine, and – nominally – to send German troops, via Petrograd and Vologda, to drive out the British. The Germans also granted recognition to Georgia and Estonia, while allowing the Bolsheviks other outlets to the Baltic. This time there was really no need to intercept any wires. On 28 August, a German newspaper reported that there had been an exchange of notes between the Bolshevik and German Governments. That night, Reilly returned to Petrograd, accompanied by Berzin, to complete the details of the rising.

On 29 August, the Cheka struck in Moscow. As a result of Marchand's disclosures, the French Deuxième Bureau Office was raided, and all French agents seized, save for Colonel de Vertement, who escaped over the roof. Hill at once broke off all contact with the French, and sent an agent to warn Reilly in Petrograd; but the agent was caught on the train. The Cheka then swooped on the ballerina Dagmara's flat, where Reilly was to be found when in Moscow. She managed to conceal two million roubles on her person; but, as the Cheka were about to leave empty-handed, Colonel Friede's sister walked in with documents for Reilly in her music satchel. That night, Colonel Friede was arrested. He was tortured, and finally confessed. But although the Bolsheviks had only discovered a little about Reilly's plot, what they did discover was alarming – was Reilly at that very moment perhaps having copies of the trade treaty duplicated for distribution as leaflets on the streets of Petrograd and Moscow? The danger was acute. Reilly must be found at all costs.

In Petrograd, Reilly had gone straight to a flat he held in the name of 'Massino' to find that Cromie had sent over a bottle of wine, and that Berzin had called, promising to return on 30 August. Reilly then discovered that some of his other Petrograd addresses were being raided, and that he was being followed. Risking all, he went straight to Cheka headquarters. An accomplice there assured him: if Reilly abandoned all his aliases save that of Commissar Relinsky of the Cheka, he would be safe. Reilly remained uncaptured.

On 30 August, Reilly's plot was prematurely exploded, not perhaps as the Bolsheviks intended. That morning, Uritsky was shot dead in front of Cheka headquarters in Petrograd by a Russian cadet, who made off on a bicycle and disappeared into a building opposite the old British Military Mission. That evening, after addressing a meeting at a Moscow factory, Lenin was shot at by a left SR called Dora Kaplan. He was carried off seriously wounded – and apparently dying.

The Bolsheviks began the Terror. Russian officers and members of the bourgeoisie were shot by the hundred. After midnight, Lockhart was dragged from his bed by the Cheka. Peters showed him the pass which Lockhart had given to Berzin. 'Where is Reilly?' Peters asked. When Lockhart refused to reply, he was arrested. On the Volga, Trotsky was drafting a wire to Lenin, when an urgent message came from Sverdlow. 'Come here without delay. Ilitch has been wounded – how dangerously is not known. All is calm.'

In Petrograd, Reilly rang up Cromie at the old British Embassy on the morning of 31 August, and arranged to meet him in a café at noon. Cromie did not turn up. That evening, Reilly decided to risk a visit to the old Embassy – but he found it already surrounded. Covered by the guns of two Bolshevik destroyers in the river, the Cheka had descended on the great house. As they battered down the front door, the British Consul dashed upstairs to destroy some papers, covered by Cromie at the head of the staircase with a revolver in his hand. As a report in *The Times* later stated, most of the old Embassy staff were in the Chancery, being paid, when suddenly 'in rushed an excited man in an overcoat and a soft hat, with Browning pistols pointing towards us in each hand, while he shouted at the top of his voice "*Rooki vverkh!* "(hands up)".' After a few moments, shots were heard. As the Cheka had begun to come up the stairs, Cromie

41

had opened fire, killing one man and wounding another. The Cheka returned the fire. Cromie fell mortally wounded, pitching headlong down the great scarlet and white staircase. As the Embassy staff were marched out, they saw Cromie's body lying at the foot of the staircase, and his blood on the second stair from the bottom, where he had struck his head. His body was then mutilated by the mob, which had surged into the mansion with the Cheka, and flung out of a second floor window. Reilly, mingling with the Cheka agents outside, vanished into the starving city.

Cromie's murder had immediate repercussions in both Russia and England. It signified the end of any British presence whatever in the old Russian capital, while in London, it was taken by some to justify any British intervention from then on: no further excuse was needed. When the news reached the War Cabinet, it was suggested that a strongly-worded telegram 'should be sent to the Revolutionary Government threatening personal reprisals against its leaders.' There had been no word from Lockhart since 17 August, when he was reported to be in Moscow. The Foreign Office had practically reached agreement with the Soviet Government to repatriate the British representatives in Moscow, when the Soviet Government put forward fresh terms. These 'inclined the Foreign Office to think that the British representatives had all been killed.' The War Cabinet decided that the Foreign Secretary should wire to Moscow 'threatening reprisals against M. Trotsky, M. Lenin, and the leaders of that Government, if the lives of British subjects were not safeguarded.'

In Petrograd, on the evening of Cromie's murder, the Bolsheviks told the Dutch Minister that they had documents 'proving conclusively' that the British were involved in Uritsky's murder. Though Lockhart was released on 1 September, the hunt for Reilly was intensified. As long as he remained at liberty, the terrible danger remained of the streets of Moscow and Petrograd being deluged with incriminating leaflets about the trade treaty. The following day, as the Terror increased in violence, the Central Committee hastily ratified the treaty. But as they were alarmed at the ominous account of the Allied plot, revealed only to a small extent by seized documents, they decided at the same time publicly to denounce the treaty as a forgery. An official Bolshevik statement was therefore issued on the same day, announcing the suppression of an Allied plot, based on bribery and forged documents, to capture members of the Central Committee, and to proclaim a military dictatorship. Reilly, it was stated, was one of Lockhart's chief agents, and had been handing out large amounts of roubles in bribes. 'Instructions were found that in the event of a successful revolt, forged secret correspondence was to be published, between the Russian and German Governments, and forged treaties were to be manufactured, in order to create a suitable atmosphere for renewing the war with Germany.' It was also agreed that this statement should be issued at greater length in leaflet form as 'agitational literature' to the advancing Allied troops.

On 3 September, this statement appeared in the Bolshevik press, with extensive revelations of a plot organised by Lockhart. 'Papers today full of the most fantastic accounts of an Allied conspiracy of which I am said to be at the head,' Lockhart recorded in his diary that day. 'The account, which reads like a fairy-tale, includes "buying over of Lett troops, shooting Lenin and Trotsky, taking Petrograd and Moscow by hunger, blowing up bridges, and appointment of dictator" not to mention the wildest and most false account of my arrest.'

Captain Hill at once sent a girl courier to Dagmara the ballerina's flat in Moscow, offering to take over Reilly's network. She was too late. The Cheka were there again. Though her story was believed, and she and the ballerina again escaped, another girl then walked in with documents for Reilly from the American secret agent Kalamatiano. That afternoon, the American was arrested (to

43

be released unharmed, many months later). Only Reilly and Hill remained free.

Next day, Peters again arrested Lockhart, whom he proceeded to treat with some leniency, even allowing his girl friend into his cell for regular visits. Peters claimed that he had organised a fictitious plot to spring the real plot within the old British Embassy in Petrograd.

The same day, Réné Marchand was induced to write an open letter to President Poincaré. The Allies, wrote this Bolshevik dupe, could only have approved of what Reilly was doing if the Bolsheviks had formed a close alliance with Germany. 'I am aware that this is actually what is currently said, and that certain Allied agents even live for the search . . . of "documents" which will establish the "alliance".' Marchand said he himself had on previous occasions suspected some complicity between the Bolsheviks and the Germans. But 'today it is difficult seriously to suppose that the Soviet Government has decided to bind its fortunes with those of the Central Powers . . . whatever should be the future development of military events, I consider it unlikely that the Soviet Government would ever resolve to call Germany to its aid . . .' Marchand had served the Bolsheviks well.

On 6 September, the Dutch Minister organised a sort of state funeral in Petrograd for Cromie. The coffin bore one large wreath from the British Admiralty. The British and Bolshevik Governments exchanged very sharp telegrams. On the same day, Reilly returned to Moscow, where photographs, rewards and warrants for his arrest, under every possible name, including Relinsky, were posted up all over the city. He eventually managed to contact Hill, who gives an impressive description of him at this desperate moment. 'Reilly's bearing, when I met him,' records Hill, 'was splendid. He was a hunted man . . . he had been through a terrible time in getting away from Petrograd, and yet he was absolutely cool, calm and collected, not in the least down-hearted, and only concerned in gathering together the broken threads and starting afresh.' At one point, Reilly even considered giving himself up in return for Lockhart. Hill persuaded him to leave Russia. While Hill obtained fresh false papers for him, Reilly was forced to lie low in Moscow. For two desperate weeks he somehow eluded the Cheka, by choosing places where even the secret police were reluctant to go. He spent several nights in a brothel, hiding in the room of a girl in the last stages of syphilis. Finally, Hill produced false papers in the name of a German, Herr Bergmann. Armed with these, Reilly managed to escape from Moscow by train in a railway compartment reserved for the German Embassy, and then from Petrograd on a Dutch tug.

The whole truth may never be known about this dark period. Bruce Lockhart's crucial diary entries for much of August will remain closed for another twenty-odd years. The Bolshevik archives will never be published; their evidence would almost certainly reveal a story of double-dealing and treachery, which would seriously violate the time-hallowed revolutionary myth. However, it can be concluded that it is quite probable that the British were somehow involved in Uritsky's murder, and that it had simply become a race as to who would strike first; and that it is more than probable that the British had nothing whatsoever to do with the attempt on Lenin's life.

The last thing that Reilly would have wished to do was to murder Lenin, and thus turn him into a Bolshevik martyr. The attempt on Lenin was most probably an immediate (and despairing) left SR reaction to the news that Lenin had now concluded *another* treaty with the hated Germans, triggered off by the earlier killing in Petrograd.

Two diary entries in Bruce Lockhart's published diary, written while in prison, give his overall view of the plot.

24 September. 'Today the *Izvestia* published the letters to Poincaré of one of the French agents, Marchand, in which he mentions a meeting at the USA consulate where the blowing up of bridges and rails was discussed.

Although I was not at this meeting and knew nothing about it, my name is still mentioned as the instigator of everything and arch-criminal. Although the meeting was said to have been presided over by (the American Consul) Poole, no mention of the Americans. For political reasons of course!'

30 September. 'Peters told me the other day that the Americans were the worst compromised in this business and that what they (the Bolsheviks) had against me was nothing. And yet not one word has been said against the Yanks!'

The Americans perhaps knew that they were badly compromised. The same day that Bruce Lockhart wrote this last entry, Poole, then on his way out of Russia, stopped off at Oslo; and there he went for a quiet talk to the British Embassy. In a 'personal and most secret' telegram to the Foreign Office, the British Ambassador wired that Poole had told him confidentially that 'there is strong suspicion that an agent named Reilly, whose wife appears to be living in New York, has either compromised Lockhart, who employed him in propaganda among Letts, by exceeding his instructions and endeavouring to provoke a revolt against the Bolsheviks, or has even betrayed him.

'Reilly advocated encouraging a revolt, but Lockhart, after consulting the United States Consul-General (Poole) and the French Consul-General (Grenard), refused to do so, and instructed Reilly to limit his efforts to propaganda with a view to deterring the Lett soldiers from resisting Allied forces. It appears that Reilly was in communication with a certain Russian strongly suspected of being an agent-provocateur, to whom he had given an address at which he still remained some days ago. Lockhart (? is now) arrested. Neither Reilly nor the Russian has been arrested, and they are still at large. Hence suspicion.'

This message reached the Foreign Office in London on 1 October. Rex Leeper (of the Political Intelligence Department, which acted as liaison between the Foreign

Office and the Secret Intelligence Service) commented thus: 'I have seen several reports from Reilly and have always found them quite satisfactory. MIIC (later to become known as M.I.6) will know all about him. It seems to me possible that Reilly, when he found the game was up and Mr Lockhart could not be saved, hid himself because there was nothing else left to do. But whether Reilly acted falsely or merely unwisely, Mr Poole's account of the story clears Mr Lockhart from the charges made against him by the Bolsheviks which have been exploited by the Germans. This would be useful to us if we wished to publish a denial of the Bolshevik story.'

Balfour, the Foreign Secretary, agreed. 'This may be most useful,' he minuted. The Russia Department added that Reilly 'will be closely interrogated when possible. This telegram does not definitely state that he disregarded Mr Lockhart's instructions. He is able to pose as a Bolshevik and obtained a passport from Litvinov.'

The matter was referred to the Director of Military Intelligence at the War Office, who in turn consulted MIIC (the Secret Intelligence Service). They sent the following written reply (which is a rarity to find in the official records) on 10 October: 'Reilly is an officer who was sent to Russia as a military agent last March. In June, it became apparent that his utility as a military agent was being impaired by the fact that he was in touch with Mr Lockhart, who was using him for some political purpose. Reilly had been warned most specifically that he was not to get into any official position, or to get mixed up with politics; therefore when it became apparent that he was doing so, a wire was sent ordering him to proceed to Siberia to report on German prisoner of war camps – this with the idea of getting him away from the political atmosphere, in which he was being involved.

'He apparently never went there; perhaps he was ordered not to do so by Mr Lockhart. He certainly had no business to be doing propaganda, which he apparently was instructed to do by Mr Lockhart.

'MIIC have all the details of this man's career, and I

47

suggest that it is advisable to wire to Sir M. Findlay (in Oslo) to advise him and Mr Poole that they should not raise a hue and cry about Reilly until we know more about the circumstances. We have had one report that it was a Lettish officer who gave the plot away; and because it has failed, it does not seem right or just that the blame should be cast on a man who should properly have never been employed on such work. Presumably the clue, to which the United States Consul-General refers, is the fact that Reilly's wife is in America. MIIC have her address, and incidentally some of Reilly's valuables and his will.'

One must comment first that Consul Poole's admission that Reilly was instructed to prevent the Lettish troops from resisting Allied troops is not far removed from encouraging outright revolt. Secondly, it may be as well to read this SIS report on Reilly and his activities with a good deal of reserve. The report claims that he was a military, not a political agent, rigidly limited to military affairs. But with all the plots and counter-plots going on in Bolshevik Russia that summer, political and military affairs had become inextricably entwined. As already stated, Bruce Lockhart's exact relationship with Reilly towards the end remains officially obscured for another twenty years. It may well prove that Reilly carried out Lockhart's advice or orders more faithfully than can at present be deduced.

Reilly himself, however, is more explicit about the role he played. New evidence came to light in 1970, when word reached the present author that the Dutchman who brought Reilly out of Petrograd was still alive. Mr Harry van den Bosch of the Hague could give an eyewitness account of some of the desperate events of the summer of 1918; he also had in his possession a hitherto unpublished letter from Reilly.

Mr van den Bosch had been a naval engineer. Before World War I, he was the Russian agent for a consortium, one of whose members was the French firm Schneider

Creusot. He became resident engineer for the construction of the naval harbour at Kronstadt. Just before 1914, he moved to Reval in Estonia, where he was appointed Dutch Consul; but he continued to have business in St Petersburg. During the summer of 1918, he was in and out of Petrograd in a tug, trying to look after Dutch residents. One night, he had a visit from a girl who asked him if he could take someone in trouble out of Petrograd in a hurry. He had had various such requests, and feared a trap. Finally, he agreed to do so, provided this person signed on as a crew member of his tug. A few nights later, Reilly arrived quietly at the quayside. He said he was a German antique dealer. Van den Bosch took him on board (for no payment, incidentally). They survived the usual search by the Bolshevik port authorities, and set sail. Reilly imagined they were heading for Helsinki, which was then neutral, from where he could get a ship to England. In fact, through a misunderstanding, van den Bosch was going back to Reval, then a German naval base.

On arrival at Reval, Reilly's false papers survived scrutiny by the German authorities. He put up at the Golden Lion hotel, having to mix with the German officers also there. He was invited to dinner by van den Bosch and his wife, who was suspicious of him. German officers were also present, but Reilly easily held his own. He badgered van den Bosch to take him on as quickly as possible to Helsinki. Finally, they left for Helsinki. On arrival at the quayside, Reilly shook him warmly by the hand, gave him a sealed package, which he told him not to open until he was out of sight – and disappeared. This was the last that van den Bosch saw of him.

He duly opened the package, inside which there was a photograph (which is on the front of this book), and a long letter in German, written on 10 October at the Golden Lion hotel at Reval:

'My dear van den Bosch,

I feel that after everything you've done for me, I must not leave here clothed in all the lies I had to use, and that

I owe it to you to say who I really am. I am neither a 'Bergmann' (ie a miner) nor an art dealer. I am an English officer, Lt. Sidney Reilly, RFC (Royal Flying Corps), have been for about six months on a special mission in Russia, and have been accused by the Bolsheviks of being the military organiser of a great plot in Moscow. The Russian papers from 3 September and later will inform you sufficiently about me. In any case, the Bolsheviks have done me a great honour: on my account they have published a special decree that foreign counter-revolutionaries will be punished exactly like Russians, and they have put a great price on my poor head. I can boast of being "the most sought after man" in Russia. If the B's had caught me, they would have shot me without more ado, for officially my Government could do nothing for me.

'I am not an art dealer, but an art collector, and can even boast of being among the experts. My Napoleonic collection is really among the biggest in the world. I have really studied in Heidelberg and am a D.Phil. I have been engaged for many years on state matters in Russia: one part of the war I was a purchasing agent of the Russian Government in Japan and America. I have an office in New York – 120 Broadway – and the greatest connections. The latter are at any time completely at your disposal. I am married, and cannot refrain from saying, to a woman whom I consider to be the most charming, the prettiest and the bravest woman in the world. My wife lives in New York, and the poor thing has heard nothing from me these last months. You can imagine what she has gone through this last month when she read of my "Moscow affaire" in the papers! The lady whom you met in Petrograd is the fiancée of one of our officers, and for me nothing more than a very dear friend who has risked much to help me. Naturally, I am now *clean* shaven, and now look – really quite respectable!

'So, I believe I have now confessed everything. You can now easily imagine how I was burning to get away from here. For:

50

1) I could easily meet someone here who knows me, and would betray me, and then it would be "for a life of rest".
2) It is of great importance that I get to London as soon as possible, and
3) I am burning to cable "my little girl" in New York.

'If it were not all so, then my stay here would really be "great fun". My colleagues – the "Herrn" enemy (ie the German officers in Reval) – have made the very best impression on me, and I carry back with me the most pleasant memory. I believe it is not necessary to stress that I consider it my duty towards *you* not to interest myself in anything military here, and not to pump the officers who were introduced to me. I believe I played the role of the art dealer Herr Bergmann quite well, only once or twice did I catch myself using an English expression; for the rest, I imagine your lady wife was a little suspicious of me! It would be useless to offer you my gratitude – it is too big.

'I suppose we will meet again. If you come to America, then you know where to go. It is very possible that I shall be busy at the peace conference in resolving the Russian question. Then we shall meet in The Hague.' (Reilly here imagines that the Peace Conference will be held at The Hague, not in Paris.) 'Of course, I do not need to tell you how very confidential this letter must still remain meanwhile; so long as the B's are still at the helm, I must ask you to preserve *absolute* silence.

'Probably I will soon return to Russia, but from the other side, and I hope that then for a change the Bolsheviks will run away.'

CHAPTER FOUR

South Russia

Back in London, Reilly's explanations were easily accepted by the Secret Intelligence Service. He was awarded a Military Cross for his highly dangerous work in Bolshevik Russia over the previous six months. But he was given little time to recover from his exertions and enjoy the fruits of victory. For the War Cabinet had decided, two days after the Armistice, to give substantial support to the anti-Bolshevik forces in South Russia. The Dardanelles (the straits into the Black Sea) were now open; and up-to-date information on the forces in South Russia was urgently required. These forces consisted of the Volunteer Army formed by General Alexiev (the Tsar's former Chief of Staff), who had now died, and been replaced by General Anton Denikin, former commander on the Western Front; and the Don Cossacks, under their Ataman (elected leader) General Krasnov, who had accepted German help after the treaty of Brest-Litovsk, and whose forces with German backing had by now reached Voronezh province, not far south of Moscow. It was felt that the Don Cossacks, who had previously in early 1918 accepted British help, would turn back again to the British. But the whole situation was uncertain. In late November, therefore, a high-powered British Military Mission under General Poole (the former commander of Archangel) set out for South Russia. Reilly and Hill were sent out separately on a Greek destroyer. Officially they were political agents (as Bruce Lockhart had been to the Bolshevik Government), lightly disguised as 'English merchants'; their reports on the South Russian scene were to be independent of those of the Military Mission.

At Sebastopol, they parted company with John Picton Bagge, the former British Consul-General at Odessa, who had accompanied them. Picton Bagge was returning to resume his duties at Odessa – a crucial post, for the French had taken it into their heads to launch a full scale military invasion of the Odessa region just after the Armistice; and the morale of the French troops was known to be poor. South Russia had in early 1918 been loosely divided into French and British 'zones' for the purpose of assisting the White Russian forces: the British had opted for the Caucasus and the Don territory, while the French had taken over the territory around the Crimea and the Odessa region, and further west.

On arrival at Ekaterinodar (capital of the Kuban province in the Caucasus, where the Volunteer Army was based), Reilly was first rather surprisingly told by the pro-Allied 'National Centre' party that Admiral Kolchak had 'already agreed' to co-operate with General Denikin. Kolchak had just launched a coup d'état in the Siberian capital of Omsk, proclaiming himself Military Dictator. Reilly reported to the Foreign Office that when the time was right, Kolchak would put his forces under Denikin's command. Reilly therefore thought that any conflict with Kolchak, who was not a military leader, could be resolved by official British recognition of General Denikin as Russian Commander-in-Chief.

The military problem of overcoming the Bolsheviks, Reilly stressed in one of his first reports to the Foreign Office, was a comparatively easy one, as they would not stand up to well-equipped regular troops. It was a case for quick, decisive action in South Russia. The question of unity of command with the Don Cossacks was nearly settled. 'General Krasnov is first and foremost an opportunist, and once he is given to understand in a most decided manner that the way to Allied support in the matter of equipment, arms, goods, etc. lies *via* Denikin, he will submit, and being a clever man, he will do so with good grace and a workable amount of bona fides . . . The (Don) Cossacks, if well supplied in the matter of equipment and armament, will follow Krasnov in a campaign against Moscow if the campaign promises to be short, but they will *not* remain in the field for an indefinite time,' warned Reilly – quite correctly.

'It will be fatal for Russia and probably for Europe if this task is not accomplished by next summer,' he went on. There was great need for anti-Bolshevik propaganda work in Allied countries; and well-known writers like Maurice Baring and R. C. Long, who knew Russia well, should be induced to help. 'Whatever the diversity of opinion may be about extending military and economic help to Russia, there can be only *one* opinion on the urgent necessity of world-wide propaganda against Bolshevism, as the greatest danger that has ever threatened civilisation.'

Reilly and Hill then both saw General Denikin, who 'is a man of about fifty, of fine presence, the dark Russian type with regular features; he has a dignified, very cultured manner, and could be classed as belonging rather to the "higher staff officer type" than to the "fighting type". He gives one the impression of a broad-minded, high-thinking, determined and well-balanced man – but the impression of great power of intellect or of those characteristics which mark a ruler of men is lacking,' reported Reilly. This is undoubtedly the best six-line description of Denikin ever made – and many such reports were made at this time.

General Denikin did not speak to them very optimistically. 'People think that in order to pacify Russia, all one has to do is to take Moscow. To hear again the sound of the Kremlin bells would, of course, be very pleasant, but we cannot save Russia through Moscow. Russia,' he emphasised, 'must be reconquered as a whole, and to do this, we have to carry out a very wide sweeping movement from the South, moving right across Russia.' The Ukrainian separatist movement under Simon Petlura, he thought, was merely Bolshevism in Ukrainian garb, and must be fought at once before it spread.

'We cannot do (all) this alone. We must have the

54

assistance of the Allies,' he stressed. Munitions and supplies would not be enough. They needed Allied troops to move behind them to hold the re-won territory, garrison the towns, and protect their rear. Only in this way could they mobilise fresh troops in newly-won territory. '*We* will do all the fighting, but *you* must stand by, and protect us from being struck in the back,' he told Reilly. Soon, he added, he would move either to the Crimea, or to Rostov, on the lower Don.

After assessing the present and future potentialities of the Volunteer Army, Reilly then went up to visit Ataman Krasnov on the Don, who seemed to think he was Louis XIV, and *l'état, c'est moi*' Reilly reported. 'Krasnov now institutes a form of Government for which the old regime in some of its worst forms supplied the inspiration and the methods.' Reilly found bribery, and gross abuse of power, particularly in the law courts. '*Ils n'ont rien appris, ni rien oublié,*' he noted bitterly. In the towns, the Donetz miners and workers were thus in constant ferment. All labour associations were suppressed which had the effect of driving the workers into the arms of the Bolsheviks, who were carrying on a strong propaganda campaign. Among the Don Cossacks, however, the disturbance had only affected the younger ones, who were tired of fighting, and wanted some loot.

When Reilly saw General Krasnov, his first impression was that Krasnov would not keep his agreement with General Denikin. For when Reilly tried to draw him, speaking of Denikin's 'wise and unselfish attitude,' Krasnov, instead of giving a banal reply, flared up. 'The institution of a supreme command over all the forces in South Russia at the present moment was premature,' he said. 'One should have waited until the military and political situation was much clearer. Everybody out there (ie in the Volunteer Army) is thinking only of grasping the maximum amount of power.' ('I could not help interposing at this,' reported Reilly, 'that I have observed it "elsewhere" also.') 'Look at the tremendous staff they all have,' Krasnov went on, 'whilst I can carry on all my work with a staff of practically two men . . .'

Reilly came away from the Don feeling that Krasnov should be chastened, but kept. (He was a 'stupid man', Reilly told a friend, 'but an impresario of genius.') If Krasnov would not respond, there was always General Bogaievsky, who was very popular both with the Don Cossacks and the Volunteer Army. But the Cossacks had become used to German speed and could understand neither the Allies' apparent slowness, nor their failure to go into the Ukraine and stop the separatist movement. (In fact, the French were trying to do just that, and meeting the greatest hostility from the local inhabitants.) Reilly warned that a strong Bolshevik blow might still make the Don Cossack army disintegrate. 'The unfortunate fact that at every visit of Allied officers the old national hymn "God protect the Czar" has been repeatedly and insistently played at the slightest pretext, has produced a deplorable impression, and is being interpreted as proof that the Allies have come to restore the monarchy . . . Things have gone so far that a legend has found credence that the Allied officers who came to the Don were Russian monarchists dressed up in British and French uniforms.'

On his return to Ekaterinodar, all Reilly now discussed with the Volunteer Army leaders was finance and the restoration of trade. Denikin's advisers stated that they must have Allied help; but Allied credits, which could be partly guaranteed by Russian gold in Allied banks, should be made to one central bank, which would call in the profusion of local currency, and issue new currency notes. All this Reilly approved in a detailed report.

Reflecting on his visit to the Kuban and the Don, Reilly considered that the Volunteer Army 'represents the only concrete dependable force and living symbol of Russian unity. It is now past its heroic period and (has) reached (the) critical point where it must either become (the) determined factor for rallying all constructive elements, or slowly but surely disintegrate. This will entirely depend upon promptitude and extent of Allied support. Although total strength estimated at 150,000, field force only 60,000.' Denikin, though, must make a political declaration. His delay over this was due to two of his senior generals, both convinced monarchists, who thought that acceptance of the moderately liberal 'National Centre' programme would antagonise their best regiments, which were mainly composed of monarchist officers. Reilly also urged that a British High Commissioner should be sent out to General Denikin.

Any modern war correspondent who has tried to assess the strength of an irregular or semi-regular force in the field, and who knows the outcome of the Russian Civil War, will recognise this as a brilliant assessment by Reilly. It is unfortunately impossible to reproduce more than a fraction of this series of accurate and perceptive reports.

On 28 January 1919, on his way back to Odessa to join Picton Bagge, Reilly passed through Sebastopol, the great naval base in the Crimea where British and French warships were at anchor. Here he found the Bolsheviks making great efforts to subvert the sailors and troops; 'money, women and all forms of entertainment are the principal means of propaganda . . . to create a feeling of home-sickness,' he reported. These efforts were having some effect amongst the French; but the Bolshevik agitators could make 'no headway at all with the British sailors.' In a further report, Reilly pressed for the return of the Black Sea Fleet to the White Russians. Just before the Armistice, the Germans had handed over most of the ships to the Ukrainians. The Allies had seized the remainder when they entered the Black Sea and sent them to Constantinople (now Istanbul). The Russians, stated Reilly, now wanted them back.

In early February, Reilly was back in Odessa, now under French military occupation and in complete turmoil. Numerous conflicting forces were milling around in the Ukraine. First, there was the French-backed Volunteer Army, which had acquired the reputation of being a group of neo-Tsarist reactionaries. Then there was the Ukranian separatist movement, effectively under the leadership of Simon Petlura, a member of the Ukrainian Directorate, which wanted autonomy for the Ukraine. There was also a Bolshevik rebel leader called Gregoriev, who was mainly after loot. Then there was the young and almost totally illiterate peasant anarchist leader – Nestor Makhno, the most successful anarchist in the field in any civil war this century. He had the knack of descending upon a town or garrison, wrecking it, and then disappearing with his followers. Sometimes he would disperse his men for a while; but he always managed to re-assemble them. Finally, there were the official Bolsheviks themselves, invading the Ukraine from central Russia. Into this maelstrom the French had stepped. Soon they found themselves in the greatest difficulties about who to back. The situation was complicated further by the presence of large numbers of German troops. These were more or less trapped in the Ukraine amidst the warring forces, and were trying to get back to Germany.

When Reilly returned to Odessa, one of the first people he met was the Polish financier Karol Jaroszynski, through whom the War Cabinet had bought control of the major Russian banks in early 1918, before the treaty of Brest-Litovsk. The Russian pre-revolutionary banks were unlike British or French banks, since they were also large financial conglomerates in their own right. They had a stranglehold over most of the Russian economy, particularly over the grain trade. If the Bolsheviks could somehow be defeated, the British would end up owning a major share of the Russian economy, as in China after the Boxer Rebellion.

Reilly decided that this project could and must be revived. He at once introduced Jaroszynski to Picton Bagge, who wired to the Foreign Office on 4 February asking for permission for Jaroszynski to come to London. But the Foreign Office, who had temporarily forgotten about the 1918 Russian bank deals, replied acidly that they had 'no reason for wishing Yaroshinski (sic) in this country.' Picton Bagge then wrote a private letter to Sir George Clerk (a senior official at the Foreign Office), in which he highly commended Reilly's reports on the Volunteer Army and the Don Cossacks; in fact, he wrote, 'with all the high Russian Generals at Ekaterinodar, Reilly is persona gratissima.'

He went on, 'I consider it of the greatest importance that Carl (sic) Yaroshinski should be given a visa for England, and every facility extended to him. His influence is enormous both in Russia and Poland, and his interests almost fabulous. He wants to have *England* behind him, and British interests demand that we should have him with us'. But as he was a great talker, 'and at least two hours are required for the overture, lunch is better than office hours, and dinner better than lunch,' he added.

On 6 February, Picton Bagge wired again to the Foreign Office that he had sent Captain Hill, to whom he had entrusted his letter to Sir George Clerk, to London the day before with all Reilly's reports; and Hill should arrive about 16 February. Having seen Reilly's reports, Bagge strongly urged that any decisions, especially about events on the Don, should be suspended until Hill reached London. Reilly, he stated, was now studying the situation in Odessa, where all the necessary information about the Ukraine could be obtained. When Reilly's work was completed in South Russia, Bagge suggested that he too return to London, unless the Prinkipo conference actually took place, which Reilly should attend as his relations with all Russians were so good. (It was President Wilson, at violent logger-heads with Lloyd George and Clemenceau over Russian policy, who had suggested that all warring Russian factions should be brought together on Prinkipo Island near Constantinople to try to iron out their differences over the conference table.) This outlandish proposal, made in the midst of a bitter civil war, had been coldly received especially by the French, who did their best to wreck it

59

from the start. So far, only the Bolsheviks had agreed to attend, providing certain conditions were met.

When Rex Leeper, of the Political Intelligence Department of the Foreign Office, saw Bagge's wire on the 16th, he minuted thus: 'As Mr Reilly was a Secret Service agent in Russia & is well-known to the Bolsheviks as such, I think his presence at Prinkipo would only cause trouble. The Bolsheviks could easily use his name in connection with the Lettish conspiracy in Moscow last summer so as to discredit our delegation in the eyes of Labour here. Otherwise as a political agent I think he has done extremely good work.'

The same day, Picton Bagge was wiring again that Reilly had now finished his work in South Russia, and was awaiting instructions. Bagge urged that he should return home to discuss matters verbally.

On February 21st, the Russia Department at the Foreign Office minuted that the question of Reilly's return had been discussed with the Political Intelligence Department. 'Mr Leeper says that Reilly told him when he left, that if possible he would try to work from Odessa up to Kiev, and then either round via Kharkov to Ekaterinodar, or else right through Central Russia up to the Archangel coast. I understand that Mr Reilly is prepared to risk his life in this venture, but that he would like some form of recognition for the risk taken.

'I submit that we should reply to Mr Bagge inquiring whether Mr Reilly considers that he can do any more useful work in Russia, and whether in his opinion he thinks it would be practicable for him to work his way into Central Russia and come out via Finland or Archangel.'

Underneath, J. D. Gregory, head of the Russia Department, added: 'I understand that Mr Reilly is one of the most useful agents we could have in Russia, and it seems a great pity he should return.' Gregory thought there should be consultation with Picton Bagge.

Sir Ronald Graham initialled this. But before anything could be done, the British Delegation at the Peace

Conference in Paris informed the Foreign Office that Reilly's attendance at Prinkipo would be useful. The Foreign Office therefore wired in this sense to Bagge at Odessa; for the present, Reilly should remain there. 'Do you think he could do any useful work in Central Russia?' they asked.

But no reply is recorded.

In Odessa, things went from bad to worse. On 19 February, Reilly wired to the Foreign Office, strongly criticising French action in the Ukraine. If their failure to defend Kiev from the advancing Bolsheviks was excusable on military grounds, there was no excuse for their subsequent negotiations with the Ukrainian Directorate, as the nature and fate of their incompetent military leader Simon Petlura had been plain months ago. After the fall of Kiev, the Ukrainian Directorate had lost all semblance of political and military power. As a moving force, Reilly stated firmly, Bolshevism was now dead; and there had never been a more opportune moment for combining all military forces in an united effort to smash it. The immediate fate of Russia, he warned, would be settled by the Allied Powers in the next six weeks. Provided ten to fifteen Allied divisions protected the territory won back from the Bolsheviks, so as to allow mobilization to go ahead, the Volunteer Army could start to clear South Russia by early summer.

But the Allies were not prepared to make such a large military commitment. The War Cabinet had decided that large quantities of British troops could not be sent to South Russia. The French were in grave difficulties, with too few troops in and around Odessa. President Wilson wanted all American troops out of Russia at the earliest possible moment.

On 21 February, Reilly wired again underlining that the root of the bad feeling between the Volunteer Army and the French Command stemmed from the French General Berthelot's demand for the creation of mixed Franco-Russian brigades under French command, in

61

which each regiment was to have thirty French officers and NCOs. The whole idea was quite impossible for two reasons. Though recruited from volunteers, the men so obtained would certainly be said to be defending class interests if they were to receive 250 roubles per month, which was four times the pay of the Volunteer Army privates. On the other hand, the French demand that the officers, who were to be re-elected by the Volunteer Army from a list drawn up by the French, were not to wear shoulder straps (a very touchy subject in the Russian Army), was absolutely unacceptable to all Russian officers.

Reilly also complained that French officers were especially tactless with the Russians. Owing to French-inspired confusion, he added, though Allied troops in Kherson and Nicolaiev (both ports near Odessa) received orders from both the French Command and the Volunteer Army at Odessa, Kherson was now in fact run by the adherents of Petlura, and Nicolaiev by the Bolsheviks. There was some hope, though, that matters might be cleared up when General Denikin met General Berthelot in Roumania, as had been suggested.

In late February, Reilly reminded the Foreign Office that General Schwartz, like many other Russian officers, was now unemployed, since Denikin refused to accept any Russian officers who had served under the Bolsheviks. Reilly urged that use be made of Schwartz in any attack on Petrograd. Schwartz had been the Bolshevik Military Commander of Petrograd in spring 1918, and had been awarded a British Military Cross for his part in the abortive Allied attempt to overthrow the Bolsheviks on 1 May the previous year.

In late February, Captain Hill arrived back in London with all Reilly's reports, which were eagerly read in the Foreign Office. 'In connection with Mr Reilly's suggestion that a High Commissioner should be appointed to General Denikin,' minuted Rex Leeper, 'I learn privately that unless some such step is taken, Mr Reilly will not stay longer in S. Russia as his present position is not satisfactory. He wants to be definitely attached to a political officer and given some status himself as Secretary, but I think it would be a very great loss if Mr Reilly left S. Russia. His reports have always been very interesting and reliable, and there is no one else in S. Russia who can give us the political information we require.'

Reilly's reports were then brought to the attention of Sir Ronald Graham, an Assistant Under Secretary of State. 'The reports are voluminous but interesting,' he commented drily. 'If, as I hope we may before long, the Allies recognize the Omsk Govt (in Siberia), General Denikin and his force, as the main instrument for the subjugation of the Bolsheviks, will become increasingly important, and the question of appointing a Commissioner with him must be considered.'

'Captain Hill,' noted the Russia Department underneath, 'promised Reilly he would send a telegram to him if he possibly could giving him information about his wife in New York.'

Rapid enquiries were therefore made, and Hill sent this staccato message back to Reilly. 'Reports sent in. Wiring fully few days. Nadine well New York.'

The French then took action in the Ukraine with disastrous results. On 5 March, Picton Bagge wired to the Foreign Office that the local French General, claiming to represent all the Allied Powers, had now come to an agreement with the Ukrainian Directorate. The text of this was forwarded by Reilly the next day. It stated that France would recognise the Ukrainian Directorate, which could retain the Russian Black Sea Fleet; France would also support the claims of Ukrainian delegates to the Peace Conference in Paris, and would prevent the Volunteer Army from coming into the Ukraine. In return, France would control the Ukrainian finances, and transport systems; French approval would be necessary for any changes in the Ukrainian Directorate; and the Directorate's Army would be attached to a new White Russian Army, to be formed under French Command, in the Ukraine. Reilly added that it had initially been agreed that Odessa, Nicolaiev and Kherson were to be considered as part of the Ukraine, in which France guaranteed that there would be no dictatorship during the Russian Civil War, but a democratic government. But these points had now been omitted.

The French were also taking over the entire economy, and had hurriedly organised a banking combine, made up of the Russo-Asiatic Bank, another Russian Bank, the Société Générale de Paris, and the Banque de Paris et des Pays Bas. 'French banks do not fear financial status of Russian banks, but intend using them to forward French interests,' wired Bagge. The French Command had also set up an Inter-Allied Supply Commission with a Russian President, but managed by a French Vice-President, to control the entire economy not only in the French zone, but throughout South Russia, including the Caucasus, through control of all the Russian cargo ships, a system of fixed prices, and the issue of certificates for all imports and exports. The Russian Cooperative Societies, the Allied Consuls, the local *zemstva* (local councils), the Volunteer Army and local financiers were all represented on the Commission; but control remained firmly in French hands. In Odessa itself, very little wheat was left. The town was practically threatened by famine, unless grain could be obtained from the Kuban; but the contractors there demanded payment in other goods; and negotiations dragged on.

The French, warned Bagge in another wire, were now in fact closely linked with the most reactionary of the Ukrainian landowners, who had been behind the Russian General Skoropadsky, the pro-German puppet leader of the Ukraine during the German occupation. The French really wanted a new puppet leader; and it was Skoropadsky's former Russian officers, whom Denikin disliked, who were to join the Franco-Russian mixed brigades. Bagge considered the whole plan very unsound and short-sighted. It was clear that if Reilly

64

was going to go ahead and win British support for Jaroszynski's banking project, he would have to move fast.

But Picton Bagge also underlined that the French military position in the Ukraine was deteriorating. Morale amongst the French troops was very low.

If there had been a definite plan, wired Reilly firmly, local Bolshevik risings could have been stopped. But now Bolshevik propaganda among the French troops was really having its effect. At Vosnesensk (due north of Odessa), a French regiment had held a meeting when ordered into action; though its officers induced it to advance a short way, it had returned to barracks when fired on. French Zouave troops abandoned their train on discovering that it was taking them to the front. The French Commander now readily admitted that his men were reluctant to fight. The local Russian General, whom Reilly thought reliable, had been assured by the French military authorities that there would be no French agreement with the Ukraine; but this, in fact, might now be concluded within a few days, and the French Chief of Staff, who had been in charge of the negotiations, boasted that his policy had triumphed. Reilly urged that this officer be removed. The Russian General preferred a complete rupture to the present state of affairs; he would withdraw from Odessa altogether, he told Reilly, advance up the Don and the Volga to link up with Kolchak in Siberia, and then return to clear the Ukraine.

There was then a disaster. The Bolsheviks attacked Kherson on 8 March and the town rose en masse. Men and women opened fire from roofs and windows on the Greek troops who were supporting the French. The Greeks suffered heavily, and only just escaped on a French ship which arrived at the last moment. A massacre followed. The Greek survivors returned to Odessa boiling with anger at the French. Events then moved quickly. The British Commander-in-Chief at Constantinople, who was much disturbed by Bagge's and Reilly's reports about Franco-Russian relations, summoned both of them for consultation. As a result, Reilly was told to return at once to London, and then go on to the Peace Conference in Paris. He was to press for the urgent despatch of a British High Commissioner to South Russia to achieve Allied unity.

At Constantinople, Reilly wired the Foreign Office, with Picton Bagge's approval, concerning what both considered to be an important point about South Russia. The French attitude towards the Volunteer Army was really caused by Denikin's harsh attitude towards all those Russian officers who had served with the Bolsheviks, or with the pro-German General Skoropadsky in the Ukraine, or with the Ukrainian Directorate. These officers now formed a large body of malcontents in Odessa, whose presence there much harmed Volunteer Army prestige. While Bolshevik officers taken whilst fighting were always shot by the Volunteer Army, former Bolshevik or Ukrainian officers had to face a Court Martial, and were usually degraded. This had just happened to two Russian Generals, who had been reduced to the ranks. One of these, whom Reilly knew personally, had rendered the British cause great service in Moscow and held the British Military Cross. All Jewish officers were disbarred. Reilly had discussed the matter fully with the Russian Generals at Odessa; and they all thought both Denikin and Kolchak should grant some amnesty. Most Red Army officers were only serving under compulsion, or to save their families from starvation, and a relatively easy way out should be made for them.

At Constantinople, Reilly and Bagge also had urgent discussions about resurrecting the Russian bank scheme of 1918. Bagge said that he would go back to Odessa, rescue Jaroszynski, and get him somehow to London, as the French adventure in the Ukraine was obviously doomed to disaster. Bagge would accompany the Polish financier to London, and put forward a new scheme for the economic regeneration of White Russia, under British control. Revitalising the Russian economy was vital, if the White Russians were to win. Reilly agreed with all this. After his trip to London and Paris, now that the Prinkipo proposal had died a natural death, he would leave immediately for the United States. He would use his excellent contacts there, gained during the war, to interest American banks and big business in Bagge's scheme. Their cooperation would be invaluable.

Reilly then left for London.

CHAPTER FIVE

The Anglo-Russian Banking Empire

Reilly probably reached London on 20 March 1919. On the same day, the Foreign Office, which had been complaining for some while about French activities in South Russia, sent a very strong note to the French Embassy. It condemned the French agreement with the Ukrainian Directorate; the agreement had evidently been made on behalf of the British as well.

In Paris, the Allied statesmen were more engaged in bitter conflict with each other than with making the peace. William Bullitt, a young American envoy sent to Moscow with Lloyd George's clandestine approval, nearly precipitated a complete breakdown when he returned to Paris with plans for a ceasefire and peace talks on Russia. Lloyd George threatened to return to London. Then came news that Bolshevism had broken out in Hungary. Finally, the statesmen patched up their quarrels; and President Wilson, Lloyd George and Clemenceau met in a series of secret sessions to try to get the German Treaty completed. The Russian kaleidoscope then shifted again: Admiral Kolchak's forces in Siberia made a major advance.

The Hungarian situation was considered potentially the most dangerous. On 25 March, the Council of Four (Italy was numbered among the Allies) decided to reinforce Roumania, and pull back from Odessa, which was to be secretly evacuated. Foch was so angry at this that he refused to transmit the necessary orders. Bullitt did not receive the enthusiastic reception he expected. As President Wilson could not see him straightaway, the American envoy came round and breakfasted with Lloyd George, who was enthusiastic. But the President, already under great strain, was 'so furious' that Bullitt had seen the British first, that he refused to have anything further to do with the matter. Peace negotiations with the Bolsheviks thus remained temporarily in abeyance in Paris.

More alarming news came from Picton Bagge in Odessa, where things were now going from very bad to downright appalling. On 28 March, however, the Quai d'Orsay informed the Foreign Office that the demands of the French Command in South Russia had now been approved; and General Denikin had been told to comply.

'But when will the question of policy in Russia be decided?' asked Sir Ronald Graham, when he saw all this in the Foreign Office on the 29 March. 'I am not at all sure that the appt. of a High Commr. in S. Russia would not be advantageous. There is a great lack of political guidance and co-ordination. But this might be discussed in Paris and Lt. Reilly can throw interesting light on the situation (he goes there tomorrow).'

On 1 April, as *The Times* printed a slashing attack on the Bolshevik leaders, the story went round in Paris that the Bullitt peace proposals were nothing but a business deal in return for Russian concessions; and this was supported by a 'sinister report' that an American bank and two German banks, had already combined for this purpose, 'the actual work of exploitation being entrusted to German engineers.' What part Reilly played in the propagation of this story must remain obscure, although it is a fact that he had arrived in Paris on 30 March. He was probably involved in it; and it did much to kill off Bullitt's proposals.

On 3 April, *The Times* took the story further. Its Paris correspondent wrote that the idea 'of a shameful "deal" with the Bolsheviks on the basis of some form of Allied and American recognition of the Lenin-Trotsky "Government", in return for economic, commercial and financial concessions . . . was fortunately scotched in the nick of time . . . But,' he warned, 'it is by no means killed and is at present lurking underground.'

Reilly may well have had a meeting with their Paris correspondent, but certainly not with *The Times* editor, Wickham Stead, who loathed all Jews and Reilly in particular.

On 4 April, the French debacle at Odessa, which had long been looming, finally came to pass. By now there was no food in the town, the Bolsheviks were advancing steadily, the clandestine Bolshevik Soviet was daily growing in influence, and the morale of the French troops was sinking lower and lower. The French General in command (without any instructions from Paris, it seems) now lost his head and ordered an immediate withdrawal. He shamefully handed the town over to the clandestine Soviet. The retreat was carried out in two days amidst appalling circumstances. Vast sums were demanded by the French to take Russians, on their own ships which the French had commandeered, across the Black Sea to Constantinople. Most of the French troops and sailors were drunk, having broken into a liquor store. Thousands of Russians were left on the quayside to the mercy of the Bolsheviks. French officers blamed the Russians for the whole catastrophe. Those Russians who did find berths were very badly treated – during the crossing, the French charged five roubles even for a glass of water.

'The French name indeed stank,' reported Picton Bagge on arrival at Constantinople with Jaroszynski; and he at once asked permission from the Foreign Office for Jaroszynski to come to London.

France's problems, however, were not over. At Sebastopol, the great naval base in the Crimea, the French Fleet mutinied. The French adventure in South Russia was now at an end. But all mention of the evacuation of Odessa was rigorously suppressed in the Allied press.

After his short visit to Paris, when he had a part in scotching the Bullitt peace proposals, Reilly sailed straight to the United States, where he was reunited with

Nadine in New York. But their meeting was not the success that Reilly evidently hoped; during his long absence Nadine had made other friends. There was even talk of a divorce. But Reilly had little time for the problems of his personal life. He had to concentrate on persuading American banks and businesses to co-operate in the Jaroszynski scheme. He was soon making the rounds of American boardrooms and meeting Presidents of the bigger corporations.

On 10 May 1919, Reilly was ready to report on his progress. In a long wire from New York to Picton Bagge at the Foreign Office, Reilly stated that American bankers and industrialists were looking to Russia both for a market and for raising capital. 'In view of diminished purchasing capacity, the intensified production and tendency to minimise imports in Europe, stagnation in the American export trade is bound to come, and they rightly hope to find equivalents in Russia.' But though Finland was actively interested, and American businessmen were already shipping some goods to Novorossisk (Denikin's main port on the Black Sea's eastern coast) and to Archangel, Americans on the whole were waiting for the restoration of order in Russia. The American International Corporation, Armour and Company and Ford, however, had already made 'tentative agreements' with the Russian financier Batolin, who had been in America for some time.

According to Colonel Raymond Robins, the former unofficial American political agent to the Bolshevik Government, Batolin was an 'able and competent (Russian) peasant banker, a grain buyer, a sort of embryo Armour, a man who had a fleet of ships on the Volga, some eight hundred agencies scattered throughout the grain regions of Siberia and the Ukraine, several banks, and an effective organisation.' Colonel Robins states that in August 1917, Kerensky, Savinkov (then Acting War Minister), Chernov (the SR leader) and Kornilov (the Russian Commander-in-Chief) agreed to appoint Batolin as a Special Food Commissioner with a member of the American Red Cross as his assistant. The Red Cross would then make an appeal to Herbert Hoover (who organised American relief) for food supplies. But Kerensky delayed the appointment until the Kornilov affair, by which time it was too late. Batolin presumably went to the United States soon after.

Reilly's report stressed his belief that the moment was ripe for an Anglo-American link to exploit the Jaroszynski and Batolin interests, each country using his own Russian financier. Reilly had thoroughly discussed the matter with Samuel MacRoberts, the Vice President and Anglophile 'Foreign Minister' of the National City Bank. MacRoberts was eager to start an Anglo-American syndicate. 'In a field so huge there can be no place for jealousy,' he had told Reilly, who wanted to bring in not only the American International Corporation, Armour and Company, and Ford, but Guggenheim, Rockefeller, Dupont and John Ryan as well. Reilly suggested that both Jaroszynski and Picton Bagge should come to New York, if the British Government agreed. Even if Jaroszynski was opposed to Batolin, Reilly still thought they could go ahead. Another consideration was that MacRoberts did not want the initiative left to J P Morgan. New York businessmen would not like this, as Morgan was so closely linked with the British Government.

On 15 May, Reilly wired to Picton Bagge again. 'Have seen Richard Martens,' (who was generally recognised as a great expert on the Russian economy). 'He has most exhaustive information, statistical maps and charts on Russian natural, industrial and commercial resources. I consider that his presence in England would be of great value in connection with any scheme for economic reconstruction of Russia. His co-operation would be especially desirable in the Jaroszynski matter. Please use your influence in obtaining for him permission to go to London.'

On the same day Reilly sailed back to England on the *SS Baltic*.

*

Above: The Rosenblum family, photographed in 1890. Young Sigmund, surrounded by his father and mother, Grigory and Pauline; and his two sisters, Elena (left) and Marie (right).

Sigmund Rosenblum, later Sidney Reilly, aged 16.

Reilly's entry form to the
Royal School of Mines.
September 1904.

City and Guilds
CENTRAL TECHNICAL COLLEGE,
EXHIBITION ROAD, LONDON, S.W.

Form to be filled up by Candidate for Matriculation, or person wishing to attend
a Complete Course of Instruction.

Name (in full) *Stanislaus George Reilly*

Age last Birthday? *27 years* (Date of Birth *24.4.1877*)

Particulars of previous education and employment in practical work

Particulars as to tenure and value of any Scholarship now held ___ *Nil*

Whether competing for an Entrance Scholarship *No*

Whether taking alternative Practical Chemistry and Physics *No*

Department the Candidate proposes to enter *Electrical Engineering*

Candidates who have Matriculated at the University of London are required to give the
following particulars:—

Date of Passing		Division	Subjects taken, in addition to English and Elementary Mathematics
Month	Year		

In the event of my being admitted as a student, I hereby undertake to conform to
the Rules of the College as printed on the back of this form.

Signature of Candidate ___

Address of Candidate *9 Porris Square, Bayswater, W.*

Signature and Address of Parent or Guardian

I am independent of both

Occupation or Profession of Parent ___

Date *Sept. 5, 1904*

Below: Reilly's entry form
to Trinity College,
Cambridge. October 1905.

Reilly's gift to his first cousin F., from St. Petersburg in 1913. The inscription
is part of the 29th stanza of the *Rubaiyat of Omar Khayyam*.

Allied invasion of Russia to suppress Workmens Revolution, and re-establish Tsarism.

Sensational plot discovered to overthrow Soviet government.

Allied complicity in counter-revolutionary plot proved

British diplomat in Moscow discovered at conspirative meeting.—Lavishly distributing bribes. Fabricating forged documents.

The following is a summary of a statement issued by the Soviet government, which discloses a widespread plot instigated by the Allied governments to overthrow the Russian revolution.

On August 14 th. at twelve o'clock, at the private room of Mr. Lockhart, the representative of the British government in Russia, an interview took place between him and a commander of one of the Soviet detatchments in Moscow.

At this meeting it was proposed to organise a rebellion against the Soviet government in connection with the British landing on the Mourman. In order to maintain close relation between the British diplomatic agents and this comm ander of the Soviet troops, an English lieutenant, Sydney Reiley was delegated to act under the alllas of «Rels». It was proposed that certain parts of the Moscow garrison should be sent to Vologda to open the road for the English, while the rest of the garrison should arrest the Council of the Peoples Commissioners in Moscow, and establish a military dictatoship.

For this purpose on Aug. 14 th. Mr .Lockhart handed 700,000 roubles to his agents. On Aug. 22nd another meeting took place at which 200,000 roubles were assigned for the purpose of arresting Lenin and Trotsky, and members of the Council of Public Economy, seizing banks, posts and telegraphs. On Aug. 28th 300,000roubles was paid over to this commander of Soviet troops who was to go to Petrograd to establish connection with the English military group working there together with a group of Russian counter-revolutionaries.

At the same time in Moscow, meetings under the auspices of the agents of the Allied Powers were held with the object of intensifying the famine. It was proposed to blow up certain bridges on the railways, and wreck food trains, in order that the population of Moscow and Petrograd should become so maddened by hunger as to rise in revolt against the Soviet government.

Letters have been discovered with Mr. Lockhart's signature on official British government paper, delegating this commander of Soviet troops to act on behalf of the British government.

The plot was discovered by the commander disclosing the whole scheme to the Soviet authorities.

Acting on this information the Soviet authorities on the night of Aug. 31st surprised a conspirative meeting at which Mr. Lockhart was present. Although Lockhart was arrested, some of the conspirators escaped and are now at large. They have carried out a portion of the ir plans. Trainloads of food were blown up by them at Voronezh. Documents were seized at this meeting which shows that the intention of the Allies as soon as they had established their dictatorship in Moscow was to declare war on Germany and force Russia to fight again. In order to find a pretext for this, a fictitious treaty between Russia and Germany was concocted which presented the Soviet government as selling the independance of Russia to Germany. This forged treaty was to have been printed and scattered broadcast.

FELLOW WORKERS!

Here is positive evidence of the real purpose for which you have been brought to Russia.

You are being used as the tools of your capitalists who are working here in close unity with the agents of bloodstained Tzarism, for the overthrow of the first Socialist Republic, and the re-establishment of the former reign of oppression.

YOU ARE NOT FIGHTING FOR LIBERTY. YOU ARE FIGHTING TO CRUSH IT.

FELLOW WORKERS !

Be honourable men. Remain loyal to your class, refuse to be the accomplices of a great crime, Refuse to do the dirty work of your masters.

G. TCHITCHERINE,
Peoples Commissary for Foreign Affairs.

The "agitational literature" issued in the form of leaflets by command of the Bolshevik Central Committee to the Allied troops advancing from Archangel.

Above: Sidney Reilly in 1918. *Below:* Sidney Reilly. Probably taken in 1925.

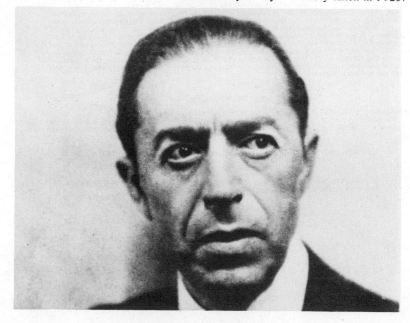

Karol Jaroszynski.

The library in the Jaroszynski Palace in St. Petersburg.

Boris Savinkov. *(BBC Hulton Picture Library.)*

Лло́йд
Джо́рдж

Свидание
в Генуе
8 марта
10 Апреля
18 Апреля?

Two rare early Soviet cartoons of Lloyd George, still considered to be the leader of the Western Alliance, showing the importance Soviet Russia attached to the Genoa Conference in April 1922, when she hoped to obtain de jure recognition.

The first cartoon depicts Lloyd George as a coy young girl in a bonnet, holding up a sheet of paper headed: "Conference in Genoa", with the dates of 8th March and 10th April crossed out, and a query against 18th April. Underneath is written: "The fickle heart of a beautiful young lady prone to treachery."

—— Сердце „красавицы" склонно к измене и к перемене...

ПАСХАЛЬНОЕ ЯЙЦО.

Лло́йд
Джо́рдж

ДЕ-ЮРЕ

The second cartoon, entitled: "Easter Egg", shows Lloyd George as a mother hen sitting on an egg marked "de jure".
Underneath is written: "The Broody-Hen of Genoa."

Генуэзская „наседка".

Исполнительный
Комитет
III Коммунистического
Интернационала
Президиум

Центральному Комитету Британской
Коммунистической Партии

15 Сентября 1924.
Москва

Дорогие Товарищи,

Близится момент, когда английский парламент приступит к обсуждению вопроса о ратификации договора, заключенного между правительствами Великобритании и С.С.С.Р. Яростная кампания, поднятая вокруг этого вопроса британской буржуазией, свидетельствует, что большинство этой буржуазии вместе с реакционными кругами выступает против этого договора, стремясь к разрыву соглашения, которое упрочивало уже между пролетариатом обоих стран и вело к восстановлению нормальных отношений между Англией и С.С.С.Р.

Великобританский пролетариат, сказавший в свое время свое веское слово, когда угрожала опасность перерыва последних переговоров, и которой принудил правительство Макдональда подписать соглашение, должен напречь максимальную энергию в дальнейшей борьбе за ратификацию и против попыток британских капиталистов понудить парламент к аннулированию этого договора.

Необходимо всколыхнуть английские пролетарские массы и привести в движение армию безработных, положение которых может быть улучшено лишь в том случае, если С.С.С.Р. предоставлен будет заем для восстановления его экономического положения и если будет налажено деловое сотрудничество между британским и русским пролетариатом. Настоятельно необходимо, чтобы группа рабочей партии, сочувствующая договору, оказала усиленное давление на правительство и

PLATE I

The Zinoviev Letter, Page 1.

эт организации группой, которая вместе, с вашими
выполнениями, может эл в момент возникновения, остро-
вой борьбы. Составьте мозг военной организации
партии.

Внимательно просмотрите списки военных ячеек, выделяя наиболее энергичных и
способных людей. Обратите внимание на тех
более талантливых военных специалистов,
которые по тем или иным причинам ленились
службу и исповедуют социалистические убежде-
ния. Вовлеките их в ряды коммунистической
партии, если они честно готовы служить про-
летариату и желают в будущем руководить
ее слепыми механическими силами, находя-
щимися на службе буржуазии но национальной
армией.

Сформируйте руководящий оперативный
орган Военной Секции.

Не откладывайте этого на будущее,
которое может быть чревато событиями и которое
может застать вас врасплох.

С пожеланием вам всякого успеха
как в организационной работе, так и в
борьбе

С коммунистическим приветом

Председатель Президиума ИККИ
Зиновьев.

Член Президиума
Мак Мануе.

Секретарь
Куусинен.

PLATE IV

The Zinoviev Letter, signed by Zinoviev, witnessed by McManus an
Kuusinen.

Immediately on receipt of Reilly's second wire, Picton Bagge sat down in the Foreign Office to write a long paper urging the formation of a banking combine. This in fact amounted to a British takeover bid for the entire Russian economy. Before 1914, he wrote, German investment in the Russian banks had made German influence predominant in Russia. After a lapse during the war, it was again predominant at the time of the Bolshevik revolution, and had increased after the French debacle at Odessa. Now that Germany was defeated in the West, and thwarted in her 'drang nach osten' towards Salonika, Constantinople and Baghdad, she would again go for Russia and Siberia. But it was important for the British Empire to be able to draw extensively on Russian wealth, and for Russian markets to provide an outlet for British goods. Since it was 'jejune to expect (that) German energies can be throttled and stifled,' we should 'check and control German political and economic activities, directing them into proper but sufficient channels. If we did this, British manufacturers would find a good market for British goods, with no competition from Russian goods, and we would prevent the otherwise ineluctable German-Russian alliance.

Bagge went on: 'I propose as a solution of the problem before us that Great Britain should secure control of the big banks in Russia, of the big transport companies, and of the insurance companies . . .' The main objective, however, was 'far more imperial. Control of the banks should mean both the economic and political control of Russia.' In February 1918, the British Government, through its loan to Jaroszynski, had secured the right to place two directors on a board of four, who would control all his banks. He and Bagge had now worked out a scheme for setting up a Central Bank or Trust, based in London, with only two directors – Jaroszynski and an Englishman. This would control all the Russian banks, which in turn dominated the grain trade, and owned most mining, mineral and timber concessions, and some transport companies. The two directors would therefore control most of Russian industry which in practice would mean the entire Russian economy. 'The British Director should not be a mere financier, but an imperially thinking man,' wrote Bagge. (It is not clear who he had in mind for this job, but it may have been Sir Samuel Hoare.)

British industries would be represented on the Russian bank boards by British subjects, who should hold both senior and junior positions in all the Russian banks and industries, since British interests had previously been much prejudiced by Russian or Jewish representation. 'As regards the younger men,' wrote Bagge,' I would suggest that they be of the public school-boy type. They should be made to live . . . with selected Russian families, with a view to acquiring the language, in which they should be subjected to periodical examinations. They should also be subject to a certain amount of discipline . . . somewhat necessary in Russia where, owing to the breadth of view taken of life and the somewhat careless regard to the morrow, young men, whose moral fibre is not strong, are apt to become rather easily demoralised.' Prominent local Russian politicians would also be so employed at good salaries, when not actually in office. The Central Bank, Bagge added, would also run an intelligence network and control the Russian press.

He also recommended that the Central Bank should obtain control of the Russian Merchant Fleet on the Black Sea, the Volga and the Caspian, and concessions for constructing and operating a Chelyabinsk-Novorossisk railway, and a Volga-Don canal. This would divert to the ice-free port of Novorossisk both the Siberian and the Baltic trade, which was likely to be under German influence; while the Volga-Don canal would provide a cheap means of transporting iron ore from the Urals 'for British industries', since the Krivoi Rog deposits (north-east of Kherson) would become extinct in 25 years. British colonial experts could also assist in the 'colonisation of Siberia', particularly in the irrigation of Turkestan and improvement of the cotton industry.

Jaroszynski, who was now in Europe, was anxious to go ahead with this scheme at once, but he insisted on prior political approval. 'Politicians of standing must have a prominent place first,' he had stated. But he could not go into details of his previous transactions with the British Govérnment in 1918, as all his documents were buried 'somewhere in Petrograd'.

Bagge thus urged the British Government to conclude an agreement in principle with Jaroszynski. The Government should help the financier to consolidate his position in the Russian banks now under his control and to take over the Azov-Don bank, the Volga-Kama bank, and the Russian Steamship and Trading Company on the Black Sea, and the two large steamship companies on the Volga and the Caspian.

Bagge enclosed the two telegrams from Reilly in New York. He also sent a report from Stockholm, dated 4 April, which stated that certain Petrograd and Moscow bank directors had agreed at a recent secret meeting (presumably in Stockholm) that all banking records up to the end of the Kerensky regime were preserved. When order was restored, it would only take a short time to put the Russian banks in order again.

On 16 May, Bagge added that Jaroszynski and a colleague had arrived in France, 'and have telegraphed to me that they will be in London in a few days.'

On 29 May, the Department of Overseas Trade (DOT), to whom Bagge had initially sent his paper, forwarded it to the Foreign Office, adding that there were several British banking groups 'thinking of invading Russia when the way is open,' the most important of which were Lloyds Bank, the London County and Westminster Bank, the National Provincial Bank, and the British Trade Corporation. But Jaroszynski should choose the group with which he preferred to deal.

At the Foreign Office, the Russia Department studied

75

it all carefully, but expressed doubts. 'It is possible that M. Jaroszynski's Banks and Companies may be very reactionary . . . It might be very inconvenient for HM Government to find that they had set going, or at least encouraged, a vast combine which was using its influence to restore Tsarism . . . Mr Bagge, referring to this point of view, said that the restoration of monarchy was inevitable. That may be so, but speaking with much less knowledge than his, I should expect the restoration if it takes place to be a brief one.'

Sir Ronald Graham saw all this on 4 June. 'This is an interesting and very important scheme and, if it is sound financially and commercially, I do not think that we should raise any objection to it on the political ground referred to. The success of the scheme must depend on the establishment of a strong central Government in Russia, whether monarchical (and I agree with Mr Bagge) or not.' The scheme should be encouraged, though without committing the British Government to anything more than a careful examination.

Lord Curzon (the Acting Foreign Secretary) saw it the same day. 'The promoter seems to be sincere,' he wrote guardedly.

On 7 June, Reilly himself came into the Foreign Office, hotfoot from New York, to see Rex Leeper of the Political Intelligence Department. He expounded his view of the current Russian situation. As the Red Army General Staff had shown 'considerable ability' and a large foreign army could not be found, the progress of the White Russian Armies was very slow. Bolshevik power must therefore be broken up in three ways from within:

1) *Russian Generals and Officers in the Red Army*. As the senior Bolshevik Military Commanders would not move against the Bolsheviks without a prior assurance of White Russian support, an agent should go to Denikin to find his price for co-operation with them; Denikin would probably

76

agree if they launched a revolt in Moscow first. The agent should then go on to Moscow, discover the right men on the Red Army General Staff, and assure them that Denikin would co-operate as soon as they moved.

2) *The Church.* As the Orthodox Church was the 'strongest force' in Russia today, and recent reports from Petrograd spoke of its increasing influence, we should show sympathy to its leaders. Bishops Anastasius of Kishinev, Ageyev and Prince Trubetskoi, who were all at the moment at Constantinople, should be brought to England, where the Archbishop of Canterbury should make a fuss of them, and promise them 'material support'. Armed with this, the bishops could go straight into Petrograd on its liberation, to stop the pogroms against the Jews, who were so prominent in the Bolshevik movement.

3) *The Ukraine.* An agent should go to Ataman Gregoriev to promise him support if he would turn against the Bolsheviks (which he had in fact already done). If Gregoriev agreed, a link could then be arranged between him and Denikin.

Rex Leeper was very impressed. Reilly, he minuted, had been an 'extremely able and reliable agent in Russia during the last year . . . and recently did very good work in the South of Russia . . . He is in touch with all kinds of Russians and is trusted by General Denikin and his staff . . . If he were successful, we should achieve much more striking results this way than we shall ever do otherwise, and I think the venture is worth attempting.' The Russia Department supported this project, and stated that the Secret Intelligence Service approved, and that Reilly was willing to go.

But Sir Ronald Graham was unenthusiastic. 'The unfavourable reports at one time current about Mr O'Reilly (sic) have been disposed of, but I should say he was rather intelligent than reliable.' He was quite

77

opposed to the proposal involving the Archbishop of Canterbury, and thought that the Director of Military Intelligence (DMI) at the War Office could be consulted on the other matters.

(Sir Ronald Graham seems to have confused Reilly with a troublesome Foreign Office official called O'Reilly, who later had to be removed in great haste from Siberia – mainly for having good ideas of his own – and banished to La Paz in Bolivia. The 'unfavourable reports' about Reilly probably refer to his unavoidable visit to the German naval base at Reval on his escape from Petrograd with van den Bosch in the autumn of 1918. It is not quite clear what 'material support' Reilly had in mind for the Russian Bishops, probably only much needed food and basic supplies. But though the Church may have been the 'strongest' force then in Russia, the peasants regarded the senior clergy as black reactionaries.)

'I agree with Sir R. Graham on both points, but am no great believer in these obscure intrigues of foreign agents,' added Lord Curzon coldly.

Curzon's remarks are somewhat foolish. Reilly's other proposals were sound and imaginative; and it was exceedingly brave of him to offer to return to Moscow, since his photograph had been plastered up everywhere, all his former aliases were known, his networks were broken up, and he had been condemned to death. Reilly's first and third proposals were now referred to the DMI. As a wire had already gone off to Denikin about his attitude towards former Russian officers serving in the Red Army, no action was taken on the first. But on 12 June, the DMI sent Philip Kerr (Lloyd George's secretary) a short, tentative paper on Gregoriev, who was causing the Bolsheviks 'considerable embarrassment', and hinted that he might be worth supporting. Lloyd George's response is not known. On 3 July, however, the DMI minuted that the 'activities of Gregoriev and other anti-Bolshevik leaders in South Russia continue unabated, and though these leaders, who are

78

merely bandits and do not stand for law and order, will not co-operate with Denikin, they are a cause of considerable embarrassment to the Bolsheviks.' Perhaps some attempt at co-operation with Denikin had been made. Gregoriev, however, was soon assassinated by the peasant anarchist leader Nestor Makhno, and his band incorporated with the local anarchists.

Reilly then sought the support of Churchill (Secretary of State for War) for the Jaroszynski proposal. Churchill was enthusiastic. On 1 July, he minuted the General Staff at the War Office: 'A conference should be held tomorrow at the War Office on the Trade possibilities in the Denikin area. Sir Auckland Geddes (President of the Board of Trade) should be invited to attend: also the Head of the War Trade Department (ie the Department of Overseas Trade) and representatives of the Shipping Controller and the Treasury. The GS (General Staff) will be responsible for making the case

a) that the permanency of Denikin's gains depends upon good trading conditions springing up behind his front, and
b) that if this opportunity is seized, British manufacturers may obtain a market in South Russia of great and lasting importance.'

At the War Office meeting, Churchill said that if Denikin was to hold the great area which he had won, the people there must be more prosperous than those under Bolshevik rule. There was thus a tremendous opportunity for Manchester, Sheffield, Leicester and other British towns to gain an entirely new market; there were millions of Russian people to be held for generations to come, and now was the time to act and gain the trade. Colonel Steel of the General Staff added that it had long been realised that the economic situation was vital in the areas won. As soon as the Black Sea was open, the GS and the DOT had done their best to restart trade in the ports. From reports, and 'very indirectly from the Foreign Office from Mr Bagge,' said Steel cuttingly, they had in fact realised that military progress was entirely dependent upon the provision of the necessary supplies; now was the time to make it a 'national' affair. General Briggs (former head of the British Mission in South Russia) said that a man with a 'clear business head' was wanted out there. General Denikin had asked Briggs to take the matter up, and had said 'that if he had tanks, corn and clothing, he could capture the whole of Russia.'

It was then agreed that the special insurance scheme was not enough. But Geddes proved obdurate: was the idea to promote trade, or simply for the British Government to make a grant? After some inconclusive discussion, Churchill hurriedly concluded the meeting by stating that for the present, three things were necessary: the right people on the spot; a committee in London to meet once or twice weekly; and suitable propaganda to encourage British companies that were interested. It was agreed that the departments represented (and the Foreign Office was not) should meet once a week.

Picton Bagge, who had represented the DOT, immediately reported back to Sir Arthur Steel-Maitland (head of the DOT, and Colonel Steel's younger brother), adding that Jaroszynski insisted on prior political sanction before proceeding any further with his big Anglo-Russian project. But they could not wait indefinitely for the Foreign Office to make up their minds.

Later that day, therefore, the DOT wrote to Colonel Steel at the War Office, emphasising that they thoroughly supported the suggestion for the formation of a committee, with executive power granted by the War Cabinet, as the existing committees were powerless. As Steel-Maitland could act for both the Foreign Office and the Board of Trade, he should obviously be the Chairman. It was hoped that Colonel Steel would impress all this upon Churchill, who would in turn impress it upon the War Cabinet. Steel needed no urging; and Churchill at once asked two senior permanent officials at the War

Office (Sir Reginald Brade, the War Office Secretary, and Sir John Stevenson, the Surveyor-General of Supplies) to take the matter up straightaway with Steel-Maitland. Thus, a plot got under way to bypass the Foreign Office.

On 5 July, Sir Arthur Steel-Maitland presided at the first committee meeting, which was attended by Colonel Steel, Picton Bagge, and two members of the Russia Department of the Foreign Office. They went straight into the Jaroszynski scheme for an Anglo-Russian industrial combine. Steel-Maitland stated that Jaroszynski said that financial interests, which were 'not friendly', were trying to edge their way into Kolchak's area in Siberia, and Denikin's in South Russia. The way to fight these people was to back Jaroszynski, and have Sir Charles Eliot (the British High Commissioner in Siberia) and the British Missions in Siberia and in South Russia, place the right men in the right place. Kolchak and Denikin should not at first be told what was happening, nor should Jaroszynski be given a direct commission by the British Government. His link with the British financial group would be sufficient credential.

A member of the Russia Department replied that there was considerable opposition to any 'Anglo-Russian regime' in Siberia, and that England had an understanding with America that Siberia was in the American sphere as regards currency. But he agreed about South Russia. A British High Commissioner should be sent out to Denikin; this idea, he reminded them, had previously been turned down. Bagge then explained Jaroszynski's ideas for Russian currency, for which Treasury approval must be obtained. Colonel Steel stressed that Denikin had agreed to cease requisitioning food and supplies. The 'ice had been broken' about inducing the peasants to accept a system of barter; he would ask Churchill about obtaining a British credit for Denikin so that Russian peasants could exchange their grain for British goods.

It was agreed to hold a 'meeting of merchants' on 11 July to tell them about transport and insurance, and to

81

assure them that Denikin would not requisition anything more. Steel-Maitland promised to speak to both Curzon and Churchill, so that the matter might be brought before the War Cabinet. He would also do his best to improve transport and distribution in Denikin's area. The meeting then broke up.

Steel-Maitland went straight off to discuss the matter with Sir Ronald Graham, who approved. 'If the scheme is economically sound,' he minuted to Lord Curzon, 'it should be worth supporting and may help to form a barrier to the economic penetration which the Germans are already organising.'

Curzon now knew that he was under pressure to give a decision.

> '*Yaroshinski*.
> Sir R. Graham. What strikes me most about this scheme is that with the exception of Mr Bagge we have no one to speak with recent and necessary authority and experience about Mr Y or about his plans. I have a recollection of Mr Y as having been a complete failure in some earlier transaction. Could we not ask Sir G. Buchanan (the former British Ambassador in Russia) or someone who knows? Again how is this network of banks and societies to be set up in a country in a state of chaos and in the hands of murderous ruffians. The scheme postulates a certain degree of order. I have an instinctive distrust of gigantic schemes which are presented at the point of the bayonet, and the promoter of which must positively have an answer because in a day or two he has to be going.'

But this was so vilely written that Sir Ronald Graham had to provide a translation for Steel-Maitland before passing it on. 'Please see Lord Curzon's minute,' he wrote hastily underneath, 'the point of which is that he must be satisfied as to the financial aspect and the status of Y before giving it his blessing . . .'

On 7 July, Steel-Maitland discussed the matter with

Stevenson and Brade of the War Office. On his return to the War Office, Stevenson minuted to the General Staff that though he approved the project, the War Office's main concern was the military necessity of enabling Denikin to provision his army; the question of supplying his rear was a secondary matter. The War Office should thus press the War Cabinet on the first point, and merely support the second which was political and economic (a somewhat short-sighted view).

Steel-Maitland himself wrote to Churchill confirming that he had seen the two officials and General Briggs. Briggs had wandered off rather incoherently into a lot of other matters. Steel-Maitland felt that the whole position of Denikin needed going into comprehensively, and someone should interview Briggs thoroughly. 'I gather,' wrote Steel-Maitland tentatively, 'that you think that Denikin ought to be sufficiently helped *if possible* to give him a chance of re-establishing a decent Government in Russia.' Churchill replied by return that he was 'going carefully into the whole matter'.

Churchill thereupon circulated to the War Cabinet a paper by Litvinov-Falinsky, one of Jaroszynski's aides, strongly urging British economic help for Kolchak and Denikin. 'If England will not give this assistance, Kolchak and Denikin will perish, and then Germany will step in,' he warned. All that was needed was British backing for the formation of a powerful organisation to restore the Russian economy. 'Owing to the nature of the activities of our banks (very different from those of English banks) all the nerves of our economical life are centred in the banks,' he wrote carefully. They regulated all Russian industry and commerce, and were thus the 'only apparatus' whereby the economy could begin to be restored. To prevent German control, it was in the British Government's interest to help combine the Russian banks into 'one powerful organisation.' No help was needed from the British Treasury, but the British Government must, 'with a full knowledge of the political importance of such a measure,' give their 'direct protection' and support to this group, to enable it to obtain the necessary private finance. Kolchak's and Denikin's causes could then be 'considered safe . . .'

Churchill made no mention whatever of Jaroszynski in this paper, or in his covering note to the War Cabinet. He simply said that Litvinov-Falinsky was a former Assistant Minister of Commerce, who had 'great influence' over the Tsar and the Grand Duke Nicholas, had helped create the Russian war industries, and was a 'strong man and absolutely non-party.'

While Picton Bagge and Reilly waited for Cabinet approval, Reilly took Jaroszynski in hand. The portly financier was not difficult to handle. A tall man, with very shiny finger nails, finicky habits and a penchant for boasting, he readily admitted that his financial position was often 'very straitened owing to the lack of ready cash.' Bagge tactfully insisted that his genius was 'essentially a creative one.'

The Department of Overseas Trade noted that Jaroszynski had now also acquired control of the Azov-Don Bank (which had big property holdings in the Rostov area, and controlled the largest platinum works in the Urals). Spurred on by the British Government official insurance scheme, the British Trade Corporation, the London County and Westminster Bank, Parr's Bank, Lloyds Bank and the National Provincial Bank had now formed the 'South Russia Banking Agency' to co-operate with Jaroszynski and exchange goods by barter through the Co-operative Societies in South Russia. But lack of transport and terrible delays in telegrams to South Russia were holding everything up. Though the War Cabinet had allocated £1 million to improve the transport, it was felt that a further British credit was needed to set things in motion.

Reilly still had enemies in the Foreign Office, however, and they were not all pleased that Jaroszynski was now firmly under the control of 'somebody called Reilly, a dangerous character who had been in the

German Secret Service.' This description emanated from a member of the Russia Department.

In mid-July, Jaroszynski, no doubt accompanied by Reilly, left his London residence at 7, Berkeley Street, and went over to Paris to meet the directors of the Russian banks, in which he had a controlling interest through the bank deals of early 1918. After these directors had formally acknowledged Jaroszynski's authority, an official agreement to this effect was drawn up and signed by Putilov (Chairman of the Russo-Asiatic Bank, which had vast concessions in the Urals, and close connections with the French Société Générale), by Chaikevitch (former Managing Director of the International Bank, which controlled the entire South Russian grain trade, and most of the Russian coal and jute trade), and by Jaroszynski himself. A council was set up with Jaroszynski as President. Other Russian banks could be brought onto the council, and Jaroszynski had the right of veto. Decisions affecting the Russo-Asiatic Bank had to have the approval of the Société Générale, and of the Banque de Paris et des Pays Bas.

Jaroszynski, in fact, was becoming more and more powerful. On his return to London, he went to the Foreign Office. It is unclear whom he saw, but the interview was described as a 'pretty unsatisfactory one', for 'the stronger he becomes, the more difficult he is to deal with.'

The Russia Department now submitted an extensive report on Jaroszynski to Lord Curzon. Sir George Buchanan (the former British Ambassador in Russia) had merely written to say that the financier was probably honest, but he had never met him. Lindley (Buchanan's former chargé d'affaires, now at Archangel) had wired that Jaroszynski was probably alright, 'but his ability seems to run on those large imaginative lines which require very close watching.' A more instructive report came from the London branch of the Moscow Merchants Bank, which had originally financed his first three sugar factories near Kiev. The leading London clearing banks and Lloyds were somewhat reticent. The London City and Midland Bank, which of course knew a great deal about him, merely stated that they knew that he controlled the Petrograd Commercial and Industrial Bank, and the Kiev Bank. Steel-Maitland added that he had discussed the scheme with Sir R Kindersley (of the Bank of England), with Frank Dudley Docker (of the London City & Midland Bank, and father of Sir Bernard Docker), with W H N Goschen (Chairman of the National Provincial Bank). All these leading London bankers first wished to have an expression of Lord Curzon's approval before committing themselves.

The Russia Department reminded Curzon that Jaroszynski was going to form a holding company, of which the Vice President, most of the directors, and half of the staff would be British; while the British banking group which he chose would have an option on providing the capital. The scope and extent of the company's activities were to be vast: 'Russia (1914), Poland (1919), Mongolia, Manchuria, Roumania, Persia' were in fact to be the boundaries of the new Anglo-Russian Empire. But Jaroszynski's condition was that the British group should contain 'one or two men of high political standing who would be in close touch with HMG.' Lord Curzon was therefore urged to inform some leading financier that the scheme was 'politically desirable', and ask him to look into the matter carefully. 'Seeing that the edifice which we have been endeavouring to erect in Russia shows signs of collapsing before our eyes,' wrote an official in the Russia Department, 'I do not think that we should miss any opportunity of using the instruments for maintaining our influence in Russia, which may present themselves . . .' Perhaps Lord Curzon might also receive him briefly, 'as M. Jaroszynski regards himself as the Napoleon of Russian finance . . .'

Sir Ronald Graham approved. 'The action that is suggested commits us very little and might, I submit, be adopted. In any case an urgent decision on the subject is very desirable.'

'I think we should not move without consulting Treasury,' wrote Lord Curzon warily. 'I am not myself quite easy about our past transactions with Mr Yaroshinski, and I am a little alarmed at the concluding para of the memo from Russia Dept. It looks to me as tho we were expected to assume a continuing responsibility. Otherwise on its merits there appears to be much to be said for the scheme and I do not doubt the bonafides of its author.'

Before the Treasury could respond, there were a long series of War Cabinets on the Russian situation. General Denikin was now surging ahead, but the question of the future remained very uncertain. Could he reach Moscow on his own? On 25 July, Sir Auckland Geddes said that the economic question in South Russia was the vital one. England alone could not develop trade in Denikin's area. At the moment, it was everywhere held up because there was no British credit. Trade could not be all on one side. The Board of Trade had recently considered the matter, and thought the best plan was an insurance scheme. It was not possible to barter if military operations were going badly. Trade would in any case be very slow. £5 to £10 per head of British credit would be needed in South Russia: and at £5 per head, this came to £300 million. A £2 million insurance scheme was simply not enough. The population in Denikin's area lacked everything, and Geddes thought there was small chance of stopping the whole thing crumbling to pieces. From the economic point of view, he urged the War Cabinet not to throw good money after bad.

The War Cabinet eventually decided to give General Denikin further support, but only for a further eight months, until March 1920. If Denikin was successful, he should after this become self-supporting.

But the essence of the Jaroszynski scheme was that it involved private finance. On 4 August, it duly came before the Treasury as Lord Curzon wished. A Treasury official noted that further negotiations with the Russian banker Denisov over the British Government's purchase of a controlling interest in the Siberian Bank in Petrograd in early 1918 were in suspense until Jaroszynski put the British Government in funds to pay Denisov. Denisov had already been paid £428,000 for these bank shares by the Treasury, and Jaroszynski was believed to be willing to take up his option (as agreed in early 1918) to purchase the shares from the British Government; but not, as his contract allowed, until 1921.

Sir John Bradbury (the Joint Permanent Secretary) was somewhat hesitant about the whole affair. 'This atmosphere is too rarefied for the ordinary official mind,' he minuted on 5 August. He saw no real objection to the Jaroszynski proposal, however, 'but we ought to see the colour of his money first . . .' He was prepared to give this qualified approval for the Foreign Office to prod the British bankers to look closely into the scheme. Next day, Stanley Baldwin (the Financial Secretary) added a large tick.

'I agree that the Treasury view should be stated as above,' minuted the Chancellor of the Exchequer on 6 August. 'Add that My L(ords of the Treasury) presume that Lord Curzon will consult the Pres(ident) of the B/T (Board of Trade) before commending the project to the Bankers.'

On 8 August, Picton Bagge had a brief meeting at the British Trade Corporation, which was interested in joining the group that was to co-operate with Jaroszynski. 'Since you left this morning,' wrote a director later that day to Bagge, 'Lord Farringdon (the President) and I have had an interview with Sir Eric Hambro.' The result was that it was agreed that the Foreign Office should now state definitely that the formation of a small British group to work with Jaroszynski was desirable; until this was done, there was really no point in approaching Barings Bank, or Frank Dudley Docker (of the London City & Midland Bank) or Philip Noble (of Lloyds Bank).

The Russia Department was not entirely satisfied. The Treasury minute 'does not advance the matter very much,' it was noted. For Jaroszynski, with his 'curious ambitions and susceptibilities', attached great importance to being received officially. Could Sir Ronald Graham see him?

'I have no objection if Lord Curzon approves,' wrote Sir Ronald Graham cautiously. 'I shall be much obliged to Sir R Graham,' replied Curzon.

But the brief interview that took place was as great a failure as the previous one. Jaroszynski had set his heart on being received by Lord Curzon himself.

But Curzon had now decided to take the plunge. On 14 August, without consulting the Board of Trade, but with the full approval of the Treasury ('I agree,' wrote Sir John Bradbury on the draft), Curzon wrote to Lord Farringdon. 'While I am unable to express any opinion as to the financial and commercial merits of Mr Yaroshinski's proposals, which must be judged in the first instance on their merits by the competent authorities in the City of London, I am told that one of his main objects is to provide this country with the means, through the control of banking institutions in Russia, to prevent Germany from reasserting the predominant position in the field of Russian finance and commerce which she had practically secured for herself before the war.

'So far as this particular aspect of M. Yaroshinski's scheme is concerned, which is, in fact, the main one which affects the Foreign Office, I need scarcely say that His Majesty's Government would welcome any assistance they can obtain which would be likely to achieve the results anticipated by M. Yaroshinski. If, therefore, you are satisfied that the scheme is financially sound, and that the formation of a British group is accordingly justified, I think I may say without hesitation that we shall be prepared to give the group such support as lies in our power.'

Lord Curzon had completely committed himself. Lord

89

Farringdon, however, now up at Glenalmond in Perth, merely replied that he would give the scheme 'closer attention' on his return to London in late August; the formation of the new Anglo-Russian Empire was delayed a further fortnight while His Lordship banged away at the birds on the Scottish moors.

All that summer and autumn, General Denikin's advance on Moscow continued apace. He was not helped by his colleagues on his right and left flanks. In Siberia, Admiral Kolchak launched a brief autumn offensive; but it only lasted a month, and by the end of September he was in headlong retreat. In the Baltic, things might have gone very differently, if there had not been such appalling mismanagement. The British were particularly to blame, for the considerable military and material support which they promised to General Yudenitch arrived too late to help his autumn assault on Petrograd. The assault began promisingly enough, but inadequate supplies and incompetent leadership soon bogged it down. The Bolsheviks rallied, and several bloody battles ensued. Then Trotsky himself appeared on the scene and Yudenitch was completely routed. Yudenitch's failure, as the Bolshevik Foreign Commissar put it, was 'a scandal for the Entente.'

As Denikin advanced, the 'South Russia Banking Agency' gradually and laboriously got into its stride. But Denikin's advances were counterbalanced by the usual inefficiency and corruption amongst his officials. The British representatives sent out, happily calling themselves true 'merchant-adventurers', got nowhere.

Just before Christmas 1919, the Bolsheviks managed to hold Denikin before Moscow. Fierce fighting took place and eventually Denikin began a steady retreat. British planners hoped he would gather his forces for another attack. But there was to be no next time. White Russian morale had broken. Denikin retreated to the sea.

In late March 1920, a force embarkation took place at

the port of Novorossisk. Many Russians had to be left behind. There was an appalling epidemic of typhus. The remnants of Denikin's army were brought to the Crimea, where General Wrangel took over. He proved a much more capable leader and actually managed to break out of the Crimea, back onto the mainland. He was helped by the diversion of the Polish war with the Red Army. But all too soon, Wrangel was forced to evacuate the Crimea. The Russian Civil War was over; and his adherents were gradually scattered all over the world.

The one person who emerged with an enhanced reputation from the Russian Civil War was Sidney Reilly. His initial reports on the Volunteer Army, the Don Cossacks and the French in Odessa had been accurate and far-sighted. If the Allies, and particularly the British, had been prepared to carry out his recommendations, then things might have gone very differently. But the British public was tired of war; Lloyd George would not back Churchill; the Labour Party, and a large section of British opinion, was resolutely opposed to interference in Russia.

CHAPTER SIX

Reilly and Savinkov

But Reilly was not too down-hearted. The Bolsheviks would not necessarily remain in power in a devastated country, after the bogey of foreign intervention, which had helped unite many of the Russian people behind them, had gone away. But in England, the constant cry was to cut official war-time expenditure. Everything came under the knife – including the Secret Service.

On 19 March 1920, with General Denikin still on the mainland, Churchill had circulated a paper to his Cabinet colleagues. Correctly marked *Most Secret*, it protested against a further reduction in money available to the various branches of the Secret Service.

'Herewith I send you (a) a secret print of the case against the proposed reduction of the Secret Service Money, and (b) a series of typewritten notes on the kind of information that is now coming steadily to hand.

'With the world in its present condition of extreme unrest and changing friendships and antagonisms, and with our greatly reduced and weak military forces, it is more than ever vital to us to have good and timely information. The building up of Secret Service organisations is very slow. Five or ten years are required to create a good system. It can be swept away by a stroke of the pen. It would in my judgement be an act of the utmost imprudence to cripple our arrangements at the present most critical time. Before such a decision is taken, I must ask formally that the matter should be considered in the Committee of Imperial Defence or by a Cabinet Committee comprising the same personnel.

'I request that the funds now asked for may be granted for the next financial year. During that time it may be possible to effect economies by combining the three distinct and very secretive organisations which exist at present, viz:

1) Sir Basil Thomson's Civil organisation (ie the Special Branch).
2) Colonel Sir V. Kell's counter-espionage organisation (ie MI5), and
3) 'C's' Secret Service (ie MI6 or the Secret Intelligence Service).

'Such a combination would be advantageous, but it cannot be brought about in a hurry, having regard to the peculiar nature of the matters dealt with and the importance of not disturbing the relationships which exist.'

Though the notes on the information then being obtained through Secret Service sources are not available, the 'secret print' against the reduction of the Secret Service estimates (which was probably approved by the Cabinet on 23 March), stated that it had already been decided to reduce them during 1919 as follows:

For Espionage: from £240,000 to £125,000.
For Counter-Espionage: from £80,000 to £35,000.
But Lord Curzon had now agreed to the Treasury demand to reduce the first to £65,000, and the second to £10,000.

Churchill stated that the General Staff at the War Office regarded the new proposal as 'dangerous'.

Espionage. On a basis of £125,000; this allowed for £15,000 for the Headquarters and general management, £4,000 for Germany (proper), £30,000 for Holland (for Germany), £5,000 for Switzerland, £2,000 for Vladivostok, £2,000 for South Russia, £20,000 for Helsinki (for North Russia), £15,000 for the Far East.

On a basis of £65,000; £15,000 for Headquarters, etc., nil for Germany (proper), £18,000 for Holland (for Germany), £3,000 for Switzerland, nil for Vladivostok, £1,000 for South Russia, £8,000 for Helsinki (for North Russia), £1,000 for the Far East.

If these cuts were made, it was pointed out, there

would be 'a great reduction in the information from Germany . . . a very large reduction in information from Russia, and in particular, the schemes for obtaining information from Moscow, which are about to mature, must be abandoned . . . Abolition of the regular Secret Service in Poland, the Balkans and Spain. The agencies working in Vladivostok and China from which good information has been obtained will have to be closed.' In fact, the General Staff would be unable to work properly if this further reduction were made.

Counter-Espionage. This service, MI5, created in 1909, discovered, nursed and on 3 August 1914, smashed the whole of Germany's spy ring in England. At the outbreak of war, its running cost stood at £6,000 to £7,000 per year. By 1918, this had soared to £100,000. Since the Armistice, this had been reduced by two-thirds, and was now £35,000 per year; and Colonel Kell stated that he could further reduce it to £30,000. But now it was proposed to reduce the figure to £10,000.

If this reduction were made, 'it will not be possible for MI5 in the future to confine itself to the detection of German agents alone . . . at least three other Powers are suspected of espionage against us, and the agents of two are now under observation. It may here be observed en passant that the Indian Government had found it necessary to create a special section of the General Staff, ranking in status with MI5's organisation, to deal solely with Japanese espionage in India.'

The paper concluded: 'Taking into consideration the present unsettled state of the world generally . . . the General Staff can only regard as folly any proposal which would tend to render ineffective a weapon of defence which no other Power is able to dispense with at the present time, and is satisfied that a reduction of the grant to such a sum as £10,000 would, in fact, result in the practical crippling of the organisation.'

It had been at the Peace Conference in Paris in 1919 that

Reilly had first met the Russian whom he most admired. Boris Savinkov was a long-standing terrorist, a brilliant novelist, the Acting War Minister in Kerensky's Provisional Government of 1917, and the man who had briefly held Jaroslavl in July 1918 in anticipation of the Allied landing at Archangel. Now, in Paris, he was a diplomat, a member of the Russian Political Conference, which acted as a pressure group for the White Russian cause.

Churchill also met Savinkov for the first time in Paris, and has left an unforgettable impression of him in his *Great Contemporaries*. Churchill was clearly mesmerised by him. 'Small in stature; moving as little as possible, and that noiselessly and with deliberation; remarkable grey-green eyes in a face of almost deathly pallor; speaking in a calm, low, even voice, almost a monotone; innumerable cigarettes. His manner was at once confidential and dignified; a ready and ceremonious address, with a frozen, but not a freezing, composure; and through all the sense of an unusual personality, of veiled power in strong restraint. As one looked more closely into this countenance and watched its movement and expression, its force and attraction became evident. His features were agreeable: but though still only in the forties, his face was so lined and crow's-footed that the skin looked in places – and particularly round the eyes – as if it were crinkled parchment. From these impenetrable eyes there flowed a steady regard. The quality of this regard was detached and impersonal, and·it seemed to me laden with doom and fate. But then I knew who he was, and what his life had been . . . (It) was devoted to a cause. That cause was the freedom of the Russian people. In the cause, there was nothing he would not dare or endure.'

Churchill goes on: 'Born in Russia with such a mind and such a will, his life was a torment rising in crescendo to a death in torture. Amid these miseries, perils and crimes, he displayed the wisdom of a statesman, the qualities of a commander, the courage of a hero, and the endurance of a martyr . . . 'M. le Ministre,' he said to me (at the Peace Conference), "I know them well, Lenin and Trotsky. For years we worked hand in hand for the liberation of Russia. Now they have enslaved her worse than ever".'

Now that the Russian Civil War was over, Reilly and Savinkov became the *de facto* leaders of the anti-Bolshevik cause. The Grand Duke Nicholas (uncle to the late Tsar) was the titular head; General Wrangel still commanded the remnants of the White Armies and their camp followers, scattered around the islands of the Aegean and at Gallipoli; but it was Savinkov, financed to an increasing extent by Reilly himself, who carried on the fight on Polish soil against the Red Army. 'This last feat was little short of miraculous,' writes Churchill. With very few funds, hardly any staff and very little equipment, with only his old friend General Pilsudski (the Polish Head of State) as protector, Savinkov had nevertheless by September 1920 collected some 30,000 officers and men, and formed them into two organised corps.

Conditions inside Bolshevik Russia were appalling. Professor George Kennan, the great American authority on Russia, has written that the Great War, the Russian Revolution and the Russian Civil War and Allied intervention, had produced a situation 'where civilisation seemed largely to have broken down, where human life was one swamp of poverty, hunger, disease, filth, and apathy – where people took on the qualities of wolves, and man often became the enemy of man in the most intimate physical sense, as in a jungle.'

In March 1921, as a communist attempt to take over power in Germany was ending in failure, the Treaty of Riga brought the Russo-Polish war to an official end. Savinkov was forced to end his operations in the Byelorussian forests, and move to Prague. Here he began to organise a 'Green Guard' movement in the west Ukraine. That same month, as it became clear that the Russian grain crop sown in autumn 1920 had failed, the Kronstadt garrison mutinied, demanding the abolition of the grain monopoly. Though the Kronstadt mutineers, after bitter fighting, were suppressed, there was then a peasant revolt at Tambov against the grain requisitions. The Red Army troops who were sent to put it down, went over to the insurgents.

As the Russian famine began in earnest, an Anglo-Soviet trade agreement was finally signed in March, which allowed limited trade between the two countries. Lenin inaugurated the 'New Economic Policy', which temporarily abandoned communist principles, and allowed the resumption of private trade, in an effort to enable Russia to recover. This, however, depended on her ability to procure capital, in the form of a foreign loan, far in excess of the proceeds from her exports. With growing unemployment in England, the Labour Party favoured recognition of Bolshevik Russia. But the City of London was much more interested in collecting past debts than in developing future Russian trade through a British loan.

Conditions within Russia grew even worse. In the early summer of 1921, the prolonged drought ruined the spring grain crop sown along the Volga, in the Ukraine and north Caucasus. By mid-July, a million Russian peasants were in flight towards the towns and rivers; many huddled in refugee camps, infested with cholera and diseases of malnutrition. The crop failure had affected an area inhabited by 20 to 30 million people. Without outside help, it seemed that some 10 million people were doomed to die before the following spring.

On 5 August 1921, Sidney Reilly wrote an important paper on the Russian situation, which 'C' forwarded to the Prime Minister. Reilly's paper was based on facts acquired from 'continuous personal contact' with the leaders of 'democratic' anti-Bolshevik activities within Russia, and represented the united views of all sections of Russian 'constructive' opinion. But all Russian information, from both Bolshevik and anti-Bolshevik sources, established:

97

1) The complete or partial failure of the crops had affected two-thirds of European Russia, as a result of which some 15 to 35 million people were 'actually starving'.

2) The Soviet Government, on its own admission, was entirely unable to cope with this disaster, which was increased by the complete breakdown of the transport system, and must assume 'indescribable' proportions during the coming winter.

3) 'The anti-Bolshevik movement all over Russia is proceeding with unprecedented vigour and is rapidly reaching a culminating point.' The sporadic peasant risings, from which no district in Russia was now free, owing to the activity of various leaders, 'of which the most important is Boris Savinkov', were rapidly merging into a general rising, 'which according to the best information appears to be inevitable by the middle of September.'

4) The Red Army, or at least the purely Russian part of it, which constituted the bulk, was in sympathy with the above movement, and could not be relied upon for suppressing either a general peasant rising 'or the gigantic food riots which have now already begun'.

5) Anti-Jewish feeling was universally strong, and any popular movement might be expected to be accompanied by pogroms 'on an unheard of scale.'

A combination of all these factors must within a short time plunge Russia 'into a prolonged period of anarchy', the consequence of which it was impossible to exaggerate, and upon which it was futile to theorise. The one remaining question was whether it was still possible to do anything to save the situation. 'Slight as these chances seem to be, they exist and therefore ought to be examined.' The Bolshevik Government had admitted the magnitude of the disaster, and its inability to cope with it, and had applied to all World Governments for

98

immediate help. 'The suspicion that the Bolshevik Government has exaggerated the extent of the disaster can be fully dismissed,' Reilly wrote, 'but on the other hand it cannot be denied that the real motive of its appeal is to enlist support for the continuance of its own existence.'

The American Government had taken the initiative in offering assistance, and there was every indication that all other Governments would join in a great international relief effort, partly on humanitarian grounds, and partly on grounds of policy. 'On the other hand, it can be affirmed that relief action based on the premise that the Bolshevik Government can remain in power must prove totally ineffective.'

For the combination of famine with the extremely critical position of the Bolshevik Government, the certainty of an attempt at a general rising, the disaffection of the Red Army, and the pogrom movement, 'must result in the violent downfall of the Bolshevik Government, and will produce a state of anarchy which will defeat every effort in the direction of international relief.'

But any relief enterprise, which must inevitably be closely connected with the partial reorganisation of transport within Russia, presupposed the existence and maintenance of an administration and Police apparatus.

The Bolshevik appeal for international help seemed to provide a 'unique opportunity' for solving the problem. The American Government had already informed the Soviet Government that it would not give relief unconditionally, 'and Mr Hoover has stipulated certain elementary conditions.' But these were 'entirely inadequate', as they did not go to the root of the problem. The conditions to be put to the Soviet Government must affect the essential issues. The objection that this would amount to political interference in the internal affairs of a Government, which had received *de facto* recognition from some European Governments, could not hold good in view of the 'extreme urgency and danger' of the situation.

99

Reilly suggested the following conditions:

1) *The complete abolition of the Cheka, and all its branches.*
'The effect of this would be magical, and would in itself go far to prevent anarchical risings, and especially pogroms.'

2) *The re-organisation of the personnel of the Soviet Government.*
'This is a very big and delicate task, but not an impossible one. Lenin, supported by his more moderate colleagues, has already indicated his intention of inviting representatives of other parties to become members of his Government. It would seem necessary to go a step further and to demand that the actual executive power passes into the hands of men of such type as Krassin and Rykov, joined and supported by representatives of those parties and organisations which command appreciable support amongst the people, such as:

The Cooperative Societies,
The Railway Workers Organizations,
The Social Democratic Party,
The Cadets,
The Right SRs,
and last, but in the extent of popular support probably the strongest,
The League for the Defence of the Motherland and of Liberty (Savinkov's non-party organisation).'

As it was intended to form a moderate coalition Government, the Monarchists, on the extreme right, and the Communists, on the left wing, should be excluded. 'The present most extreme Bolshevik leaders, such as Lenin, Trotsky, Zinoviev, Radek, Kamenev, Litvinov, etc, etc, should be barred from the direction of affairs, though they should be guaranteed personal immunity.

'The situation is so critical, the danger so real, that I am fully convinced and have reason to aver that for the first time in Russian history an agreement between these various organisations and parties is possible.' The position in Russia today could be compared in one respect to that in January 1917 when the appointment of a responsible Cabinet would have saved the Monarchy, and prevented Revolution.

3) *The immediate transfer by the Soviet Government of all available cash reserves, gold, platinum and valuables to establish an 'inviolable' Trust Fund abroad, to guarantee the international credits which might be granted later.*

Desirable as relief action might be from the humanitarian point of view, it would prove totally inadequate to cope with the Russian situation. According to very moderate estimates, 7 million tons of grain would be required to feed the starving population (which by the end of the year would number up to 35 million) on a most reduced scale of rationing. At least 3 million tons of grain would be required for seed in order to ensure a moderate harvest the following year. No relief action could provide this. 'Only an immediate bold policy of international credits based upon a guarantee fund, and upon the issue of a Trade Warrant currency for Russia, can cope with the evil to any sufficient extent.' It was incidentally obvious that the transfer of the cash reserves would cripple the most undesirable activities of the Bolsheviks both within and outside Russia, namely the Third International (ie the Comintern) and its propaganda bureaux.

4) *'Unrestricted freedom and the utmost assistance' for the International Relief Commission and the Economic Commissions, which might be sent to Russia.*

These International Commissions would naturally fall into the position of 'practically administrating Russia', and would of course be supported by the 'new moderate Government', especially as under the circumstances, politics would have to cede the first place to economics for some time to come. 'The Soviet Government will not accept these conditions without demur.' But the concessions which the Soviet Government had already made during the previous six months would have seemed

101

'fantastically preposterous' only a year before. The 'essential political act' was to proclaim these conditions immediately, making it clear to the Russians that they were for the benefit of the Russian people. The 'most direct' policy was to take advantage of the 'tremendous dissension', which was already dividing the Bolshevik leaders, and to back up the more moderate section of them, 'more especially a man like Krassin.'

But there is no indication that Reilly's paper had much effect on the Prime Minister.

Churchill was still intrigued by Savinkov. On 5 December 1921, the British Embassy in Helsinki wired the Foreign Office that the Finnish Government had that afternoon received a note from Moscow 'couched in very strong language.' 'Soviet Government protest against appeal made to League of Nations regarding Karelian rising as League consists of group of nations hostile to Russia, notably France and Japan. Appeal is considered as an hostile act violating treaty of peace. Russian Government possesses proof the Finnish Government had long prepared movement and were only waiting for favourable moment to act; this is shown by the fact that attacks took place in communes touching Finnish frontier. Finnish Government is said on November 22nd to have given Savinkov permission to enter Finland and has also permitted acts of aggression by corps of counter-revolutionaries who participated in Kronstadt rising.'

The Soviet Government insisted on the Finns closing the frontier, 'cessation of all support of organisations or individuals preparing acts of aggression against Russia . . . dissolution of all organisations and bureaux on Finnish territory which directly or indirectly participate in organization of incursions . . . dissolution of all organisations formed by Russian counter-revolutionaries and expulsion of those who directed them.'

Unless this was done, the Soviet Government would take 'other steps'.

A copy of this wire reached the Colonial Office next

day, where Sir Archibald Sinclair minuted to Churchill, the Colonial Secretary: 'Another illustration of the prestige of Savinkov in Russia! Kerensky, Goutchkov, Wrangel and innumerable Monarchist groups are all scheming and agitating to bring about the fall of the Soviet and all come in for a certain amount of Bolo abuse. But whenever there is a rising, a burst of anti-Bolo propaganda, the derailment of a train or a big strike, the Bolos see the hand of Savinkov.

'He has had a good deal to do with the Karelian rising, but only indirectly through Elvengren. Undoubtedly, however, he has won for himself the foremost place in Russian opinion among the opponents of Bolshevism.'

Churchill agreed, and forwarded both documents to the Prime Minister. 'See Sinclair's note about Savinkov,' he minuted in red ink. 'He is the only man who counts.'

Churchill, in fact, now thought that the Bolshevik Revolution had run its course, and was about to produce its Bonaparte in the person of Savinkov. Shortly after, the Prime Minister asked Churchill for information on the Russian situation, and Churchill took Savinkov to Chequers. 'The scene upon arrival must have been a novel experience for Savinkov,' Churchill writes. The Prime Minister was surrounded by a band of Welsh singers, who had travelled all the way from Wales; and for several hours they all sang Welsh hymns.

When they eventually had their talk about Russia, the Prime Minister was not in a belligerent mood. He remarked that revolutions, like diseases, ran a regular course; that the worst was already over in Russia; that the Bolshevik leaders, confronted with the responsibility of government, would drop their communist theories, or would quarrel among themselves, and fall like Robespierre and St Just; that others, weaker or more moderate, would succeed to their places; and thus, by successive convulsions, a more tolerable regime would be established.

Savinkov did not like this at all. 'Mr Prime Minister,' he said in his formal way, 'you will permit me the honour

103

of observing that after the fall of the Roman Empire there ensued the Dark Ages.'

Soon afterwards, Churchill received a paper, from an unknown source, which gave Savinkov's impression of his visit to London, and to the Prime Minister in particular. 'Zeidler (a Russian Red Cross delegate in Paris) had an interesting talk with Boris Savinkov, who related how he had been to London at the request of Churchill. The latter told Savinkov that in England there was a very strong anti-Bolshevik party, which was working against Lloyd George's efforts to bring about normal relations with the Bolsheviks.

'Nonetheless, Savinkov was asked to have an interview with Krassin (the Bolshevik trade delegate). Savinkov agreed, and met Krassin at the house of an Englishman. After dinner, the host left Savinkov and Krassin at the table. The interview lasted till two o'clock in the morning, and was opened by Krassin, who said: 'We are perishing, we cannot deal with the approaching catastrophe.' Further, Krassin stated that in view of the fact that the Bolsheviks could not hand over the power to anyone, as they did not see any suitable persons who would be capable of replacing them, they were desirous of negotiating with the emigrants, and with Savinkov in particular, he being known as a revolutionary and democrat, and therefore making it easier for the Bolsheviks to explain away to the masses their desire to enter into a coalition with him.

'When Savinkov asked Krassin: "You mean that you are inviting me to come and serve you?", the latter answered: "Not to serve, but to form a coalition." To this Savinkov answered that he was unwilling to enter into any negotiations, and would always consider the Bolsheviks his enemies. That was the end of the interview.

'Prior to his departure from London, Lloyd George expressed a desire to see him, and Savinkov visited the latter by car – sent by Churchill – at a place some 300 kilometres from London. Lloyd George received Savinkov quite privately in his family. Savinkov found

104

Lloyd George singing together with other members of his family. The singing continued in Savinkov's presence, and especially for the latter's benefit, Lloyd George and family sang: "God save the Tsar". (!) After dinner, Lloyd George conversed with Savinkov for about four hours, during which time he surprised Savinkov by his knowledge of the situation in Russia.

'Savinkov stated that he had never before got so tired as in this conversation with Lloyd George, as he felt that when Lloyd George asked him questions, he knew everything about what he was asking. Nevertheless Savinkov succeeded in answering all the questions he was asked. Lloyd George also talked on the situation in general, but did not stop on anything in particular; consequently Savinkov states that he did not get a single definite thought from Lloyd George.

'When Savinkov was leaving Lloyd George, Churchill who was accompanying him said: "Do not put too much trust in Lloyd George, he is first a nationalist, but one also meets in him a desire for personal gain, and the elections play a part in this".'

Churchill sent this paper on to the Prime Minister. 'This will amuse you,' he wrote.

Although some Governments did help with food supplies to combat the Russian Famine, conditions in Russia continued to be appalling. On 31 March 1922, Thomas Jones (the Assistant Cabinet Secretary) sent this report on the conditions to the Prime Minister.

'Col. Sydney James came to see me today just back from attending the European Sanitary Conference at Warsaw. He is no alarmist and was for years familiar with epidemics in India, and is a high authority on the spread of disease. He asks me to impress on you that economic reconstruction on the Western frontier of Russia is utterly impracticable unless the present epidemics now raging on that frontier are scotched. He regards this as the very first item in reconstruction as the flight hither and thither of swarms of people terrified by the fear of infection and a ready prey to disease because of their starving condition makes stable trade conditions impossible. Commercial travellers, for example, fear to move about in these areas.

'In January this year, disease and destitution increased so rapidly that the frontier sanitary cordon between Russia and Poland broke down, and by today numerous villages and towns in Poland are in the grip of epidemics (typhus, relapsing fever – a disease which like typhus is carried by lice – and cholera). Cholera is now spreading rapidly in the Ukraine, and is a real danger in the Black Sea ports and to Europe. James himself spent four days in various frontier stations. I won't harrow you with the photographs he has shown me of what he himself was witness.'

In spring 1922, after the Rapallo Treaty was signed between Germany and Russia, Russian debts and claims were endlessly discussed by the British, French and Russians at various conferences; but little progress was made. Savinkov and Reilly continued their terrorist activities, and narrowly missed assassinating Chicherin (the Bolshevik Foreign Commissar) and other Bolshevik officials in Berlin on their way back from the Hague Conference. Savinkov was now being subsidised by various Governments to continue terrorist activity against the Bolshevik Government from his base in Prague with his 'Green Guards' – an activity which was to continue until late 1923. He was, however, becoming generally disgusted with émigré politics after his interview with Lloyd George in early 1922. Savinkov felt that Russian salvation could only be achieved through the Russian peasant masses and the Red Army. Reilly agreed with this view, but considered it essential to obtain the backing of powerful European and American groups, like Deterding (the oil magnate) or Henry Ford. He also felt it was vital to prevent the removal of the economic blockade of Soviet Russia, and to stop the Bolsheviks obtaining any foreign loan.

106

CHAPTER SEVEN

The Trust

In the late summer of 1921, a senior Bolshevik official called Yakushev, on his way to a lumber conference in Oslo, stopped off at Reval on personal matters. He was friendly with a lady who had fled to Reval, and wanted her husband to grant her a divorce. While at Reval, he contacted Commander Boyce (head of the Russian section of the SIS) and had a talk with him. He claimed that Bolshevik officials, like himself, were really bitterly opposed to the Bolshevik regime; they were what Lenin called 'radishes' (ie red outside, white within). Under their influence, Yakushev said, Bolshevik rule was changing. He then left for Oslo. Boyce was impressed: and promptly informed a friend in Berlin of this news, which was in turn passed on to the Russian emigrés there. From Berlin, the news soon reached Moscow.

As there were few Bolshevik officials travelling via Reval to Oslo, Yakushev was immediately identified. On his return to Russia, he was promptly arrested by Commissar Kiakowski of OGPU counter-intelligence (the successor of the Cheka). He was confronted with Boyce's letter to Berlin, and condemned to death. Now Kiakowski was close to Felix Dzerzhinsky the dreaded head of the OGPU. He was a former Polish agent, and Dzerzhinsky, also a Pole, liked to be surrounded by his compatriots. Together, they concocted a plan.

Early in 1922, Kiakowski (calling himself Kolesnikov) came from Moscow to Reval to see Commander Boyce on behalf of his 'good friend' Yakushev. He confirmed Yakushev's statement of the previous autumn. Kolesnikov was even more sanguine about the situation in Soviet Russia than Yakushev had been. The monarchist movement was better organised than ever. In fact, the main problem now was not so much communism, which was on the way out, but the 'wildcat activities' of certain White Russian secret agents. These might do more harm than good, as they had no real knowledge of the ever-changing situation, and might act at cross-purposes with the anti-Bolshevik groups inside Russia. But such resourceful and daring men could be of the greatest value, provided their missions were organised in concert with the underground, which had its agents everywhere and alone could elude the inevitable reprisals of the OGPU. Kolesnikov then outlined a detailed system of clandestine liaison between the monarchists both within and outside Russia, together with intricate security precautions against OGPU agents-provocateurs. He urged Commander Boyce to recommend these measures to his White Russian friends.

On his return to Moscow, Kiakowski put a proposition to Yakushev in his death cell. To obtain the peace which Russia desperately needed, they needed not only a 'New Economic Policy', but a new foreign policy as well. Renewed intervention must be stopped by pretending that communism was gradually being undermined from within, and that any outside shock would stop this process. A Latvian agent called Opperput was then put into Yakushev's cell. They were tortured, made to witness horrifying scenes of execution, and finally agreed to cooperate with their captors.

By mid 1922, the OGPU had set up the necessary 'legend' to manage and control the 'Monarchist Union of Central Russia' (MUCR), whose existence within Russia was coming to the attention of the Russian emigré groups. This 'legend' was to serve a double purpose for the OGPU. Inside Russia, it would help identify and channel towards the OGPU those really dangerous agents who would otherwise remain undetected. It would also enable the OGPU, by rigging a dispute about a tougher or weaker policy within the MUCR, to identify its real hard-line opponents. Outside Russia it could neutralise emigré groups, control western and White Russian agents and propaganda coming into Russia, and distribute careful 'disinformation' from OGPU sources.

By late 1922, the OGPU had gathered together enough agents by its various methods, and Yakushev was released from his death cell. In November, he went to Berlin as a representative of the MUCR at a Russian Monarchist Congress. Communism, he said, had failed in Russia; and the New Economic Policy (NEP) was a first concession of defeat. The MUCR had infiltrated the Secret Police. What they needed from outside was not active assistance, but moral and financial support. He strongly urged coordination. The MUCR was camouflaged as the 'Moscow Municipal Credit Association', a commercial firm which was allowed to trade abroad under NEP regulations. It could therefore obtain funds through trade; and messages could be passed both in and out of Russia. The MUCR would be known as The Trust.

Yakushev made a good impression. All this was what the White Russian emigrés believed, and wished to hear, for few at this time thought their defeat final. They considered that the Kronstadt mutiny and the growing anti-Bolshevik reaction abroad heralded the turning of the tide. All that winter much information came out of Russia via The Trust, mainly to the effect that Russia was stirring against Bolshevik rule.

In spring 1923, Yakushev travelled abroad again and complained of White Russian timidity in refusing to send an emissary into Russia, which, he said, was causing a deplorable impression in the underground movement. He also showed increased interest in Wrangel's military organisations. In the late summer of 1921, Wrangel had moved the remnants of his troops, still in their military formations, from Gallipoli and the Aegean to Yugoslavia and Bulgaria. He appointed General Kutepov as head of a 'Combat Organisation', whereby picked men could be trained for infiltration into Russia and acts of sabotage against the Bolshevik regime. Wrangel also appointed General Klimovitch as his chief of intelligence. In June, General Klimovitch came from Belgrade to Berlin to meet Yakushev and establish contact with The Trust. Klimovitch reported in glowing terms; and Wrangel, though still suspicious, instructed Klimovitch to keep in touch with Yakushev. The latter also made a good impression on another White Russian General, von Monkevitz, who was close to Kutepov. Wrangel grouped all the White Russian veterans into the 'Russian Armed Services Union' (ROVS) and proper military organisation, of a sort, was introduced.

Early in 1924, the Grand Duke Nicholas summoned General Kutepov to Paris from Yugoslavia, and put him in charge of all underground political work within Russia. Wrangel was dubious about this appointment, as he felt that Bolshevism would now have to run its course in Russia, and no terrorist tactics would pay off. Kutepov, moreover, though a first rate officer, had no experience of intelligence work; he was headstrong, and in Wrangel's opinion had a limited view of the wider implications of the Russian situation.

Kutepov, soon after his appointment, made contact with The Trust, in which he came to believe implicitly. Soon, all White Russian secret messages into Russia were passing through The Trust; messages sent from Paris or Berlin often received replies from Moscow within a week. Yakushev was received by the Grand Duke Nicholas himself, and managed to exploit the differences between Wrangel and Kutepov. Through Generals Klimovitch and von Monkevitz, he set up links with Western intelligence services, for whom The Trust supplied much information, and from whom The Trust received considerable amounts of money.

After the decisive defeat of German communism in 1923, hopes for the imminent spread of Bolshevism abroad were finally crushed. Lenin was dying. Stalin (who had become Secretary General of the Communist Party in April 1922) formed a triumvirate with Zinoviev (the head of the Comintern) and Kamenev to debar

Trotsky from the succession on Lenin's death. But the regime remained very weak. In spring 1923, when Britain's Foreign Secretary Lord Curzon sent an ultimatum to Moscow threatening to break off even *de facto* relations unless various matters were settled within ten days, the Bolsheviks hurriedly complied. This pushed the Labour Party further towards recognition of the Bolshevik regime.

At this time, affairs were not going well for Reilly. Shortly before Cumming died in early 1923, Reilly asked his chief to be put on the permanent staff of the SIS. Reilly's request was refused, and he was deeply upset. By now, his funds were very low after his long support of Savinkov; he was even selling his Napoleonic collection. He did, however, feel able to marry again – this time to a young actress called Pepita Bobadilla whom he had met in Berlin.

In January 1924, as Lenin died, Britain's first Labour Government, led by Ramsay Macdonald, recognised Soviet Russia – without insisting on a prior settlement of debts and claims, which could thus, it was hoped, be more easily resolved. But Macdonald's parliamentary position was weak; his majority in the House of Commons depended entirely upon Liberal support. He therefore asked for a Russian delegation to come to London to settle matters; after which, Ambassadors could be exchanged and a loan arranged.

In Moscow this news was greeted with cautious enthusiasm. It was decided to send a delegation to London, as a loan was desperately needed. But the Soviet position was now even weaker. It was felt that a new Savinkov terrorist campaign, coupled with the factional fight for power on Lenin's death, might seriously threaten the Soviet Government. The liquidation of Savinkov was the obvious solution. The OGPU caught Colonel Pavlovsky, Savinkov's main agent in Russia, tortured and broke him. Savinkov then received a message from Pavlovsky that a large uprising against the Soviet Government was being planned. The first blow would be struck in Geor-

111

gia, which the Bolsheviks had recently seized. Savinkov's arrival in Russia would be the signal for the uprising to begin.

The Russian Delegation duly arrived in London in the spring to discuss debts and claims. The talks lasted much of the summer, until finally, a commercial treaty was agreed: the Russians would settle their debts, in exchange for a guaranteed loan in the region of £30 million: but the debts had to be settled before the loan was made.

In June, Savinkov received an invitation to return to Russia from some of the Soviet leaders – from Kamenev and Trotsky, according to Churchill, but this can hardly be true; it was said that if he agreed to return to Russia and stand a mock trial, he would receive an immediate amnesty and be given a good position in the Soviet administration. In July, Savinkov received a more pressing message from Pavlovsky. Time was running out, and the plotters could not delay. Twenty thousand roubles were enclosed for Savinkov's expenses. Reilly was then in New York and travelled especially to Paris to warn Savinkov not to go. But Savinkov had decided. On 10 August, he set out for Russia, via Berlin and Warsaw. He was arrested by the OGPU at Minsk on the 20th. 'It seems incredible that with his knowledge of these men,' writes Churchill, 'and of what he had done against them, Savinkov should have entered the trap. Perhaps it was this very knowledge that betrayed him. He thought he knew their mentality, and trusted to the perverted code of honour of conspirators. It is even possible that truth was mingled with falsehood in their snares. Anyhow they got him.'

On 29 August, the Soviet press announced that Savinkov had been arrested, tried by a Soviet court on 27 and 28 August, and had recognised the Soviet regime. This was followed by reports that he had been condemned to death, reprieved to ten years in prison, then acquitted and freed. On 3 September, *The Times* printed an account of Savinkov's trial, which stated in part:

'Savinkov is reported to have expressed "unspeakable hatred" for Entente politicians, who subjected him and others to indignities, and considered only their own interests, while officially pretending to "assist our faithful ally". He objected in particular to Mr Churchill's calling General Denikin's forces on one occasion "my army". In another part of the evidence, Savinkov is reported as saying: "Churchill really tried very hard to help, but France gave me only words." Mr Lloyd George, he said, shuffled a lot and tried to wash his hands of the matter, and leave decisions to Mr Churchill. Savinkov is also reported to have said that before the Cannes Conference, Mr Lloyd George said he would recognise the Soviet Government on three conditions: it must recognise small private property, it must guarantee personal liberty, and it must hold free elections.'

The same day that this report appeared in *The Times*, Reilly decided to write to Churchill, enclosing a letter he had written for publication.

'Dear Mr Churchill,

The disaster which has overtaken Boris Savinkov has undoubtedly produced the most painful impression upon you. Neither I nor any of his intimate friends and co-workers have so far been able to obtain any reliable news about his fate. Our conviction is that he has fallen a victim to the vilest and most daring intrigue the Cheka has ever attempted. Our opinion is expressed in the letter which I am today sending to the *Morning Post*. Knowing your invariably kind interest I take the liberty of enclosing a copy for your information.'

In his letter to the *Morning Post*, Reilly complained of the 'suggestion that Savinkov's trial was a "stunt" arranged between him and the Kremlin clique, and that Savinkov had already for some time contemplated a reconciliation with the Bolsheviks.' This, Reilly claimed, was not so. 'Contrary to the affirmation of your correspondent, I was one of the very few who knew of his intention to penetrate into Soviet Russia.' The only source for Savinkov's alleged statements at his trial was the Bolshevik news agency. This, of course, would be swallowed by the Communist press, 'but that the anti-Communist press should accept those palpable forgeries for good currency is beyond comprehension.' Reilly remarked that Savinkov's 'confessions' revealed that 'not a single new and really confidential fact as regards Savinkov's activities or relations with Allied statesmen during the last two years has come to light.' The inference to be drawn was that Savinkov had been killed crossing the Russian frontier, and a mock trial had been staged with a Bolshevik agent impersonating Savinkov.

To this, Churchill replied on 5 September from Chartwell.

'Dear Mr Reilly,

I was deeply grieved to read the news about Savinkov. I do not, however, think that the explanation in your letter to the *Morning Post* is borne out by the facts. The *Morning Post* today gives a fuller account of the procès verbal, and I clearly recognise the points we discussed at Chequers about free Soviet elections, etc. You do not say in your letter what was the reason and purpose with which he entered Soviet Russia. If it is true that he has been pardoned and liberated, I should be very glad. I am sure that any influence he could acquire among those men would be powerfully exerted towards bringing about a better state of affairs. In fact, their treatment of him, if it is true, seems to me to be the first decent and sensible thing I have ever heard about them.

'I shall be very glad to hear anything further you may know on the subject, as I always thought Savinkov was a great man and a great Russian patriot, in spite of the terrible methods with which he has been associated. However it is very difficult to judge the politics in any other country.'

The *Morning Post* duly published Reilly's letter in full on 8 September. But when more evidence was available about Savinkov and his trial, Reilly swung right round, and wrote again to the paper in savage terms that it 'established Savinkov's treachery beyond all possibility

114

of doubt. He has not only betrayed his friends, his organisation, and his cause, but he has also deliberately and completely gone over to his former enemies. He has connived with his captors to deal the heaviest possible blow to the anti-Bolshevik movement, and to provide them with an outstanding political triumph both for internal and external use. By this act, Savinkov has erased for ever his name from the scroll of honour of the anti-Communist movement.' The fight, however, would go on.

This brought another letter from Churchill at Chartwell, dated 15 September.

'Dear Mr Reilly,

I am very interested in your letter. The event has turned out as I myself expected at the very first. I do not think you should judge Savinkov too harshly. He was placed in a terrible position; and only those who have sustained successfully such an ordeal have a full right to pronounce censure. At any rate, I shall wait to hear the end of the story before changing my view about Savinkov.'

Meanwhile, Savinkov was given a comfortable two-room apartment in the Butyrki prison, where he wrote letters to Reilly and others, received the foreign press, and went for drives in a motor-car. All the time he kept pleading with Dzerzhinsky, reminding him of his promise of release in exchange for complete confession.

In London Reilly was wondering how to strike back at the Bolsheviks. The chance came sooner than expected.

CHAPTER EIGHT

The Zinoviev Letter

All this while, Comintern documents began to appear in intelligence circles, many routed through an 'anti- Bolshevik secret service', based in Paris. In June, C. D. Westcott (the American Consul in Paris) received a photographic copy of the minutes of the Comintern, for 2 March 1924. It is a Russian text, in Reilly's handwriting, which itself purports to be a copy of the original. One passage is of particular interest:

'The Executive Committee of the Comintern, having listened to the reporters and, in view of the considerations presented by the Commissars of the Section, decreed the following:

1) Not to hasten the organisation of Communist Sections in Parliament. To warn the English Labour Party that support of communists will be terminated immediately if the Cabinet adopts imperialistic methods with respect to India and the Union of Soviet Republics. To support by all permissible means the proposed strike in the textile and mining industry, as well as in maritime transport; and to allocate therefore 10,000 pounds sterling immediately and 7,000 pounds sterling per month thereafter. To allocate to the communist press and to 'Worker's Weekly' 5,000 pounds sterling under the supervision of Comrades Stewart, Carson and (Ellen) Wilkinson.'

These minutes, whose authenticity must remain in doubt, went on to elaborate plans for sabotaging elections in France, Germany and the United States and allocated sums of money for this. A particular beneficiary was the American Federation of Labour.

The scene now shifts to Berlin, in the late summer of 1924, where many White Russian émigrés were living a precarious existence. Among them was Alexander Gumansky. One day, Gumansky burst into the apartment of his friends, Alexis and Irina Bellegarde, to say that he had just received a request from 'a person in authority in London', to concoct a forged letter, allegedly from Zinoviev (head of the Comintern), to the British communists, which would wreck the Anglo-Soviet treaty negotiations. Gumansky, it now appears, was probably encouraged to do this by the Poles, who were more eager to cripple the Soviet regime than anyone: they had just conquered a considerable part of Russian territory in the closing stages of the Russo-Polish war, and had no wish to see a strong Soviet Government, which would want to take it back. The Polish General Staff was in possession of such a document, it seems, from the Comintern; but it does not appear to have been in such a form as could be passed to the British secret service. A certain Captain Paciorkowski, attached to the Polish Embassy in Berlin, had therefore approached Gumansky, a plotter of zeal and talent, to prepare such a forged letter.

Gumansky and the Bellegardes, all young people, were thrilled at the idea and went to work with a vengeance. They managed to steal just one sheet of Comintern paper from the Soviet Embassy in Berlin. With the help of another friend, who specialised in forging people's signatures, Zinoviev's signature was added at the bottom. Gumansky took the letter away, and almost certainly gave it to Captain Paciorkowski. He appears to have added a few embellishments and sent it, via clandestine channels, along the anti-Bolshevik underground. Here, it came to the notice of Reilly, probably in early September.

Reilly was desperately looking at this moment for a

117

weapon with which to strike back at the Soviet Government, after the capture of Savinkov. Properly corrected and adjusted to British and Comintern conditions and standards, the 'Zinoviev' letter would not only wreck the Anglo-Soviet treaty, but, if released at just the right moment, bring down the Labour Government as well. He did not have much time. This is a translation of the letter he wrote in Russian from the Executive Committee of the Comintern to the Central Committee of the British Communist Party; he dated it 15 September, the very day that Churchill had sent him his second letter about Savinkov:

'Dear Comrades,

The time is approaching for the Parliament of England to consider the Treaty concluded between the Governments of Great Britain and the SSSR for the purpose of' ratification. The fierce campaign raised by the British bourgeoisie around the question shows that the majority of the same, together with reactionary circles, are against the Treaty for the purpose of breaking off an agreement consolidating the ties between the proletariat of the two countries leading to the restoration of normal relations between England and the SSSR.

'The proletariat of Great Britain, which pronounced its weighty word when danger threatened of a break-off of the past negotiations, and compelled the Government of Macdonald to conclude the Treaty, must show the greatest possible energy in the further struggle for ratification and against the endeavours of British capitalists to compel Parliament to annul it.

'It is indispensable to stir up the masses of the British proletariat to bring into movement the army of unemployed proletarians, whose position can be improved only after a loan has been granted to the SSSR for the restoration of her economics and when business collaboration between the British and Russian proletariat has been put in order. It is imperative that the group in the Labour Party sympathising with the Treaty should bring increased pressure to bear upon the Government and Parliamentary circles in favour of the ratification of the Treaty.

'Keep close observation over the leaders of the Labour Party, because these may easily be found in the leading strings of the bourgeosie. The foreign policy of the Labour Party as it is, already represents an inferior copy of the policy of the Curzon Government. Organise a campaign of disclosure of the foreign policy of Macdonald.

'The IKKI (Executive Committee, Communist International) will willingly place at your disposal the wide material in its possession regarding the activities of British Imperialism in the Middle and Far East. In the meanwhile, however, strain every nerve in the struggle for the ratification of the Treaty, in favour of a continuation of negotiations regarding the regulation of relations between the SSSR and England.

'A settlement of relations between the two countries will assist in the revolutionising of the international and British proletariat not less than a successful rising in any of the working districts of England, as the establishment of close contact between the British and Russian proletariat, the exchange of delegations and workers, etc, will make it possible for us to extend and develop the propaganda of ideas of Leninism in England and the Colonies. Armed warfare must be preceded by a struggle against the inclinations to compromise which are embedded among the majority of British workmen, against the ideas of evolution and peaceful extermination of capitalism. Only then will it be possible to count upon complete success of an armed insurrection. In Ireland and the Colonies, the case is different; there there is a national question, and this represents too great a factor for success for us to waste time on a prolonged preparation of the working class.

'But even in England, as other countries where the workers are politically developed, events themselves may more rapidly revolutionise the working masses than propaganda. For instance, a strike movement, repressions by the Government, etc.

119

'From your last report it is evident that agitation-propaganda work in the army is weak, in the navy a very little better. Your explanation that the quality of the members attracted justifies the quantity is right in principle, nevertheless it would be desirable to have cells in all units of the troops, particularly among those quartered in the large centres of the country, and also among factories working on munitions and at military store depots. We request that the most particular attention be paid to these latter.

'In the event of danger of war, with the aid of the latter and in contact with the transport workers, it is possible to paralyse all the military preparations of the bourgeoisie, and make a start in turning an imperialist war into a class war. Now more than ever we should be on our guard. Attempts at intervention in China show that world imperialism is still full of vigour, and is once more making endeavours to restore its shaken position and cause a new war, which as its final objective is to bring about the break-up of the Russian Proletariat and the suppression of the budding world revolution, and further would lead to the enslavement of the colonial peoples. "Danger of War", "The Bourgeoisie seek War", "Capital fresh Markets" – these are the slogans which you must familiarise the masses with, with which you must go to work into the mass of the proletariat. These slogans will open to you the doors of comprehension of the masses, will help you to capture them and march under the banner of Communism.

'The Military Section of the British Communist Party, so far as we are aware, further suffers from a lack of specialists, the future directors of the British Red Army.

'It is time you thought of forming such a group, which together with the leaders, might be in the event of an outbreak of active strife, the brain of the military organisation of the party.

'Go attentively through the lists of the military "cells" detailing from them the more energetic and capable men, turn attention to the more talented military special-

120

ists (ie former British officers) who have for one reason or another, left the Service and hold Socialist views. Attract them into the ranks of the Communist Party, if they desire honestly to serve the proletariat, and desire in the future to direct not the blind mechanical forces in the service of the bourgeoisie, but a national army.

'Form a directing operating head of the Military Section.

'Do not put this off to a future moment, which may be pregnant with events and catch you unprepared.

'Desiring you all success, both in organisation and in your struggle.

With Communist Greetings.'

Underneath were written the names of Zinoviev, MacManus (the head of the British Communist Party, then in Moscow); and Kuusinen, the Secretary.

This Russian text was first deciphered as being in Reilly's handwriting by the present author, and was authenticated by Mr John A. Conway, who was also shown a copy of Reilly's last letter to his wife, a photocopy of which she published in 1931. Mr Conway writes: 'I have compared these two texts and am satisfied from the quality of the writing – that is pen control and spacing, the letter formations and sizes and other characteristics – that they were written by the same person.

'Particularly noticeable are similarities in the pen strokes in the capital "D" and small "d" characters. The formation of "t" is also very distinctive, as are the "r", "g", and "f" characters. The fact that the texts are in languages with differing alphabets makes for some difficulty in comparison, but the design and drawing of characters are the same. None of the similarities taken alone would constitute proof, but the combination makes me expect them to be peculiar to the handwriting of one person.' (See the *Sunday Times*, 15 February 1970.)

Reilly's problem now was to get the letter published at just the right time: there had been rumours that there would soon have to be an election. If the letter were published at the psychological moment of the election campaign, it would ensure that the Labour Party would lose. The Conservatives would return to power and annul the Anglo-Russian treaty. Soviet Russia would get no British loan. Reilly knew that he would have to show the letter to 'C' first. 'C' was now Admiral Sir Hugh Sinclair, who had been second-in-command to the legendary Admiral Hall, the war-time Director of Naval Intelligence. Hall was a past-master on the question of timing, since it was his handling of the notorious Zimmerman telegram which had effectively brought the United States into the Great War.

There is every reason to believe that Reilly's standing with the new 'C' was very high, but he was not a member of the SIS. He could not be sure that, even if he vouched for the letter, 'C' would publish it. Reilly decided to wait a little.

He did not have to wait long. On 8 October, the Labour Government was defeated on a confidence motion. There would have to be an election. Reilly appears to have gone straight to 'C' with the Russian text, and probably a translation as well. His story would have been that either he had broken into British Communist headquarters, and copied the letter, or else – more likely – that an obliging double-agent had brought the letter out for him to copy. He would have said that he had had to work quickly, and had simply transliterated some of the Russian initials, not translated them.

But he vouched for the authenticity of the letter; and this, coming from a man with Reilly's record, was enough for 'C': the letter was genuine. The English version was at once passed to the Foreign Office where it arrived on 10 October, a Friday; and nothing was done about it over the weekend.

But Reilly also launched a little private campaign to make sure that the letter was published. On 8 October, he also contacted an old MI5 man, Donald im Thurn, who was now a director of one of the Russian émigré

122

steamship companies in the City of London. This is Donald im Thurn's diary entry for that day:

'Met X (ie Reilly) by appointment at his request. Wanted to tell me that his old enemy Apfelbaum (Zinoviev) had boasted in Moscow a few days ago that he was entering on a great propaganda war in England and Germany as the cause was apathetic and wanted rousing. He said that he had already sent instructions over here to be used as soon as the Treaty was signed. He rather feared that the present Government would fail soon, if so, it would be up to this end to decide what they were to do. Asked X to find out if this had been received, and if so, by whom.'

Reilly had chosen his man well. Im Thurn was all agog, and treated this news as a call to arms. For the next three days, Reilly gently led him on, giving him a little more news each day. On Saturday, 11 October, he asked for a little more time to 'dot the i's a bit more'; he should have definite news on Monday, 13 October. (This expression, 'dot the i's', appears to have been a favourite phrase of Reilly. He uses it in two consecutive letters to Commander Boyce, on 25 and 30 March 1925.)

On 13 October, 'C' appears to have had an important interview at the Foreign Office with Sir Eyre Crowe, the Permanent Under Secretary of State. (Ramsay Macdonald, the Prime Minister, also held the post of Foreign Secretary.) He appears to have shown both the Russian text, in Reilly's hand, and the English translation to Crowe, and told him that they were genuine. Not only a protest, but publication was discussed. Both men knew that the Labour Government was trying to abolish the intelligence services. The Russian text could not be left with the Foreign Office, as too many of the staff, particularly in the Russia Department, knew Reilly's handwriting all too well. Only the English translation was left at the Foreign Office.

That same day, Reilly gave Donald im Thurn sufficient information to convince him that he must take some action. Reilly told him what the instructions in the

123

letter were and that it had reached London about 25 September. It had been seen by at least one MP, Jimmy Maxton, the Clydesider on the left wing of the Labour Party. Maxton had shown it to Christian Rokovsky, the Russian chargé d'affaires, who had cursed Zinoviev, in front of Maxton, for being such a fool for sending such a letter at this moment. Reilly also said that Ramsay Macdonald himself and Arthur Henderson (the Home Secretary) had already heard of the letter's existence.

All this was complete invention by Reilly. If Maxton did know about the letter, he would certainly have told other MPs. It was all, in fact, 'fortifying gossip', as it has been well described in Lewis Chester's book. Reilly contacted im Thurn again on 14 October. On 25 September, he said, Macdonald had seen Arthur MacManus, the British Communist leader to whom the letter was addressed, and asked him if he had heard from Zinoviev recently. MacManus, said Reilly, refused to answer. Macdonald had then said that if he had indeed heard from Zinoviev, it would be fatal to let the news leak out at this moment. Again, all this was invention by Reilly, and dangerous invention, because MacManus was at that time in Moscow. His name had been added to the letter, along with those of Zinoviev and Kuusinen. The letter was in fact addressed to the Central Committee of the British Communist Party. But Reilly had successfully implanted in im Thurn's mind that the Labour Government might be trying to conceal the letter. Im Thurn decided to re-establish contact with his old friends in MI5. 'Saw A', he writes in his diary that day, 'who did not commit himself either way . . . but thought he had original or photographic copy.'

Events began to move faster. On Tuesday 14 October, the Foreign Office was just registering the letter as having arrived, and having a preliminary look at it, when an urgent message came from Crowe's office. Crowe said he had already seen a copy and considered it extremely important: there should not only be a protest, but publication of the letter as well. A suitable minute was therefore written, and the letter was sent to Macdonald. The Prime Minister eventually received it, in its red box, about midnight on 15 October, in a hotel room in Manchester. He wrote back to the Foreign Office that they must make sure the document was genuine: that he favoured publication in principle; and that a letter of protest to Rakovsky, strongly worded, should be prepared for his consideration. Macdonald's instructions reached the Foreign Office on 17 October.

On 15 October, Donald im Thurn decided that he must approach Conservative Central Office and the Treasurer as well – Reilly had also asked for £10,000 for his efforts, though this is not recorded in the diary. He made the contact with the Treasurer, Lord Younger, through a friendly MP, Major Guy Kindersley. Younger, a former Party Chairman and a brewing magnate, realised the political implications all too well when he met im Thurn. When im Thurn spoke delicately of a 'guarantee against loss' to the tune of £10,000, Younger arranged the whole matter over lunch. That afternoon, the two men had another meeting, this time with the Party Chairman himself. Things were quickly agreed. The Conservative Party would provide £7,500, im Thurn having let it be known that £2,500 would be provided by an (unspecified) 'relation of mine'. The strategy, they decided, would be to publish the letter in *The Times* when it would have maximum political effect. Meanwhile, Donald im Thurn would continue to try to find out who in Whitehall actually had the letter.

A further meeting that day with A, of MI5, produced no results. A did not know who had the letter. 'C must have only copy,' he wrote in his diary. 'Dangerous try C,' he added. 'Try and draw Scotland Yard first.' This produced no results either. 'Saw Scotland Yard to find out if Departments had seen letter. Answer No,' he wrote on 16 October. It was clear that 'C' had not circulated the letter. 'Must fix attention on forcing circulation,' he writes. If it was circulated, it would mean

125

that it was officially recognised. Then he could approach *The Times*. But until it was circulated, he could do nothing. A further meeting that evening with A of MI5 was more promising. He definitely offered to give im Thurn the letter if it came into his hands. 'A offered publish it through me in a perfectly safe manner. K interested.' (K was Colonel Kell, head of MI5.)

Donald im Thurn was now beginning to panic. The election was on 29 October, only thirteen days away. He had less and less time. He decided to see the Director of Naval Intelligence (DNI) to discover if he knew about the letter. The meeting on 18 October was partly successful. The DNI implied that he had seen the letter. Im Thurn also succeeded in harassing the DNI. One of his officers told im Thurn later on 18 October: 'DNI seems to think I have copy.' The officer urged him not to publish it yet: he would see the DNI again that afternoon, and be in touch on Monday morning. Although Donald im Thurn was sure that 'C' still had the only copy, he was now in high spirits. It was believed in Whitehall that he had a copy as well. 'All X's reports seem true after all,' he wrote excitedly. Reilly had indeed chosen a good bloodhound to prod his master into circulating the letter. Im Thurn went to Conservative Central Office to say that the letter would soon be published. The Tories made due preparations.

On Monday 20 October, im Thurn had another meeting with A of MI5, who said that his master, Colonel Kell, was ill and had retired to bed. Before doing so, he had spoken to 'C', who had resisted pressure from Kell to circulate the letter. 'C asked K to leave letter with him one week,' was the message im Thurn was given. This, it has been inferred, was to allow Sir Eyre Crowe, at the Foreign Office, to handle the matter in his own way, and publish the letter as he saw fit. But im Thurn's diary for that day also contains this entry: 'A thought that as C knows outside person (ie im Thurn himself) knows about letter he would cut short the week.'

But next day, all Donald im Thurn's doubts were

swept away. He had a telephone call from 'C' himself. 'C rang up to tell me about circulation. It would take place. At least, he meant me to understand that.' Now im Thurn was exultant. He told Conservative Central Office immediately. They were poised for action. That evening, A of MI5 confirmed 'C''s statement; circulation was indeed taking place. Next day, he went to see the political correspondent of *The Times*, told him the story, and advised him to check it out through his own sources. Publication was now inevitable.

All this while, the Prime Minister and Crowe were continuing their official discussion about what to do with the letter. At the Foreign Office, Crowe was quite satisfied with the letter's authenticity. He sent the amended draft of a letter of protest to Rakovsky, the Russian chargé d'affaires, back to Macdonald, observing that it could be published as soon as it had been delivered to Rakovsky. On 20 October, the draft and Crowe's minute were sent off to Macdonald's election headquarters in Wales; but he had by then moved on to the Midlands. Macdonald did not see the papers until late on 22 October – by which time the publication of the letter was inevitable.

Reilly had taken other precautions as well as hiring Donald im Thurn as his bloodhound. Just before the protest was made to Rakovsky, reports C. D. Westcott (the American Consul in Paris), copies of the Zinoviev letter, both in Reilly's hand in Russian, and English translation, were circulating simultaneously in Europe in intelligence circles, one of which reached Westcott himself. It is thus logical to assume that C's agents on the continent would have reported this news back to C, which may well have influenced his decision to circulate the letter in Whitehall. Reilly's handwriting, of course, would not be recognised in Europe.

By 22 October, other people were stepping in to make sure of publication. That evening, Admiral Hall, the former DNI, telephoned Thomas Marlowe, a friend and the editor of the *Daily Mail*. He missed Marlowe, and left this message: 'There is a document in London which you ought to have. It shows the relations between the Bolsheviks and the British Labour leaders. The Prime Minister knows all about it, but is trying to avoid publication. It has been circulated today to Foreign Office, Home Office, Admiralty, and War Office.'

Next day, Marlowe began making contacts. He had two visitors: the first said he would send Marlowe a copy; the second arrived with a copy in his pocket, but he had a friend to consult before he could agree to publication by the *Daily Mail*, and this friend's decision would not be known until the following day.

On 24 October, everything was regularised by the Foreign Office. Crowe received Macdonald's revision of the protest note to Rakovsky. He decided to send it to Rakovsky immediately, and to publish the text of the protest and the letter itself; the official explanation was that the Foreign Office had learned (through Admiral Hall, or 'C' himself) that the letter was about to be published by the *Daily Mail*. Unless it was now released, the Government would be accused of withholding it. The Prime Minister was not informed of these decisions.

The Zinoviev letter was finally published, under banner headlines, on Saturday 25 October – just four days before the election, so as to have the maximum effect on the floating voter. Immediately, Lord Birkenhead, Lord Curzon, Churchill and other leading Tories attacked in what has been described as 'a well-briefed chorus'. The astonishing thing was that Ramsay Macdonald, with the Sunday papers at his disposal, made absolutely no comment; he was either too exhausted or, as the Tories said, too embarrassed to speak. The damage had been done. Reilly and Pepita promptly left the country for America.

The Tories romped home in the General Election. Next day, Donald im Thurn was writing to his friend the MP,

Major Guy Kindersely. 'My "relation" was as good as her word – bless her. I am transmitting every penny this afternoon by cable.' This, of course, referred to the sum of £2,500. It is of interest that Conservative Central Office conveniently forgot to pay im Thurn the promised £7,500. So Reilly got only £2,500 for the Zinoviev letter. (Another interesting point is the identity of im Thurn's 'relation' – the suspicion must be that it was one of the intelligence services that Macdonald was threatening to disband.)

Furious denials came from Moscow: the letter was a forgery from start to finish, and Zinoviev had not even been in Moscow on the day in question. The new Foreign Secretary, Austen Chamberlain, easily dismissed these claims. He curtly informed Rakovsky that the information at the British Government's disposal 'leaves no doubt whatsoever in their mind of the authenticity of M. Zinoviev's letter'. This evidence could not be revealed, he told the House of Commons, for reasons 'of safety to individual life'. (In other words, Reilly's handwriting would be recognised.) The new Prime Minister, Stanley Baldwin, supported this. The authenticity of the letter had been considered by a high-level Cabinet Committee, the House of Commons was told on 10 December; the committee was unanimous that the letter was genuine. Baldwin firmly rejected demands that documentary evidence to support the decision should be given to the House.

And yet there is evidence from what the Polish Prime Minister said, after it was all over, that Zinoviev had sent instructions somewhat along these lines at about this time, probably a little earlier. 'The instructions contained in the alleged letter actually came from the 3rd International in Moscow, and our General Staff was in possession of them,' he told a colleague. 'They were used in the form of a "letter". Details appropriate to British conditions and Zinoviev's signature were added.' But this also provides evidence that he was unaware that it had all been rewritten by Reilly.

*

The forging of the Zinoviev letter was the high-water mark in Reilly's whole career. 'Whatever its impact on the (British) election, the Letter also marked a dénouement in Soviet relations with Western Europe for several years, and probably deferred United States recognition of the Soviet Union as well,' writes William E. Butler, an American scholar.

But the Soviet Government had a shrewd idea who was behind it all. With Savinkov caught, Reilly became the Soviet Union's principal target.

CHAPTER NINE

The Undiscovered End

Back in the United States, Reilly was kept busy managing his own affairs and seeing to it, by articles, lectures and more direct methods, that the Soviet Government did not succeed in getting a loan from Wall Street.

At Reval, where his friend Commander Boyce was stationed, more and more news came out of Soviet Russia that The Trust was growing in strength. A certain Marie Schultz and her husband (two of General Kutepov's best agents) told him that it now included members of the Soviet Government itself. Boyce had no doubts about Marie Schultz's information. By early 1925, he felt that the moment at long last had come to strike, owing to the growing dissension among the Soviet politicians after Lenin's death. On 24 January, Boyce wrote a heavily disguised letter to Reilly in New York. 'There may call on you in Paris two persons named Krasnoshtanov, man and wife. They will say they have a communication from California, and hand you a note consisting of a verse from Omar Khayyman which you will remember . . . If the business is of no interest, you will say: "Thank you very much. Good day."

'Now as to their business,' went on Boyce, more enigmatically. They represented a group, which would probably have a big influence in future in Europe and America; and although they did not think the matter would fully develop for two years, 'circumstances may arise which will give them the desired impetus in the near future.' It was a very big affair. It should not be talked about because other persons, who could make no headway, would much like to know who was behind it. Two parties were especially interested. There was a strong international group, who would like to wreck it, as they feared that their financial interest would be jeopardised if it succeeded. There was also a German group; but the organisers, represented by the above couple, would have nothing to do with them, for the Germans would try to take control. They had therefore linked up with a smaller French group, which was less ambitious. But they feared that they could not handle it alone, as the matter was so big. 'They are therefore wanting to enter into negotiations with an English group, who would be willing to work in with the French group.' But control would remain with the originators. 'They refuse at present to disclose to anyone the name of the man at the back of this enterprise. I can tell you this much – that some of the chief persons interested are members of the opposition groups.'

Boyce hoped that this scheme would replace the disastrous Savinkov project. 'Incidentally, you would help me considerably by taking the matter up,' he wrote. 'The only thing I ask is that you keep our connection with this business from the knowledge of my department as, being a Government official, I am not supposed to be connected with any such enterprise.' But Boyce well knew Reilly's perseverance, 'and I know also you will look after my interests without my having to make some special agreement with you.'

Reilly replied from New York in early February. 'I am kicking myself for not being in Paris, and thereby missing the Californian couple.' He fully realised the importance of such a scheme, and was in constant touch with various émigré groups in different countries. Since the failure of the Savinkov project, and the fight for political control within Russia, Reilly was convinced that the initiative must come direct from the Russian opposition. The members of the opposition must soon see that, unless they sacrificed much of their original ideas and came down to earth, they would get no support from within or outside Russia. Whether the Russian opposition now realised this, he did not know, 'and, therefore,

I regret so intensely missing the Californians.' But from his 'very intimate knowledge' of the emigrés in France, Germany and England, Reilly was convinced that the Californian couple would waste their time in negotiating with them.

'To these people the process of competition seems to be more important and vital than the achievement of mutually beneficial results.' The best person for them to see was Goutchkov, who was very energetic and was, 'as I positively know,' very well regarded by the Russian opposition. Reilly had no faith in the former Tsarists or the more recent counter-revolutionaries. They could be brought in when 'something very definite' had been agreed with the Russian opposition, but the later the better. The Russian opposition certainly knew all about internal Russian conditions, and what would be required. What they probably lacked was money and an agreement with leading foreign statesmen. 'Without such an understanding, very carefully and with great discretion arrived at in advance, the eventual reorganisation cannot possibly rest on a solid basis, especially from a financial point of view.'

The necessary finance could only be found in America, and only by the presentation of a 'very definite and very plausible scheme,' and 'very substantial proof' that the Russian opposition would act within a reasonable time. If this proof could be provided, an approach could be made to Henry Ford. 'Once his interest is gained, the question of money can be considered solved.' As for foreign statesmen, only one man was really important, and that was the 'irrepressible Marlborough' (ie Churchill), with whom Reilly had always remained on good terms. 'His ear would always be open to something really sound, especially if it emanated from the minority interests (ie the anti-Communists),' wrote Reilly. 'He said as much in one of his very private and confidential letters to me.' Reilly, in conclusion, urged the couple either to come to America, or to write to him.

On 9 March, Boyce wrote again to Reilly from Reval,

enclosing a letter from N. N. Bunakov in Helsinki (a
former British agent, and now one of The Trust's most
important agents in Helsinki). Reilly should reply to
Bunakov's questions, and ask for any further information he might want. He should also send a further letter
which Bunakov could show to the Moscow Centre,
showing that Reilly was interested in the 'commercial
proposition'; he was welcome to make any suggestions
he wished and, if possible, write something to indicate
that he could help them. 'This letter is not so important;
what is chiefly wanted is a letter from you to NNB which
he can produce so that he can show that he is working on
the matter.'

Reilly replied to Boyce on 25 March that the letters
from Helsinki were very interesting, but, as usual, were
too vague; he would reply direct. He thanked Boyce for
his 'extremely valuable estimates'; but this information
and these connections were no use, unless they 'generate
action . . . I cannot sufficiently impress upon you how
indifferent everybody has become everywhere towards
this particular business.' For seven years, promises had
been made, and nothing had happened. 'Only *action* can
arouse them out of this indifference.' He would write to
Bunakov that the first thing to do was for the Syndicate
publicly to proclaim its existence and policy, so that the
world should know that there was another Government
which could rule Russia. This would create the right
atmosphere abroad. 'Much as I am concerned about my
own personal affairs which, as you know, are in a hellish
state,' wrote Reilly, 'I am at any moment, if I see the
right people and prospects of real action, prepared to
chuck everything else and devote myself entirely to the
Syndicate's interests. I was 51 yesterday, and I want to
do something worth while, whilst I can. All the rest does
not matter.' He was grateful to Boyce for bringing the
matter to his attention. He felt sure that, if they were
dealing with the right people, they could work out
something, not only of the greatest general interest, 'but
possibly also of the greatest advantage to ourselves.'

On 30 March, Reilly wrote to Boyce again with a letter for Bunakov enclosed. He had written, he admitted, rather bluntly. 'I am sick and tired of this continuous theorising. What I propose would put the organisation immediately into the forefront of the entire movement, and make an end of the entirely useless emigrant factions, who singly and severally are discrediting the cause everywhere.' The greatest difficulty was representation abroad, as he could think of no one man who would be accepted unquestionably. At present, the chief figure was General Kutepov, whom Reilly thought a fine and honest man, 'but is he not very intimately identified with the Monarchists? I surmise that the tendencies of the Central Organisation or of, at least, some of its members are towards Monarchism. Personally, I have nothing against it, under certain circumstances and conditions, but I would consider any definite association with Monarchism at the present stage as absolutely fatal as far as foreign moral and material support is concerned – I think that the representation ought to consist of three men; it would carry more weight, and it will be easier to find three more or less suitable names than one ideally suitable . . .'

On 4 April, Reilly wrote to Boyce again that he had that day received a copy of the Syndicate's letter of 15 March to Bunakov. The letter contained an 'anticipated negative answer' to some of Reilly's proposals to Bunakov, enclosed in Reilly's letter to Boyce of 30 March. But Reilly agreed with the Syndicate that the best thing was for him to 'come out and inspect the factory personally.' He could come as soon as he had settled his affairs in New York. But he would only go into Russia after 'very thorough consultation' with Boyce and Bunakov; while there was no limit to the help he would give, 'I would naturally hate to provide a Roman holiday for the competitors.' But a successful inspection by himself, followed by a 'fully substantiated technical report,' would make a considerable impression in the right quarters.

135

In June, Boyce wrote that he had completed arrangements for Reilly to meet The Trust. But Reilly delayed his departure, citing his business activities in New York as the reason.

Meanwhile, Savinkov was still languishing in the Butyrki prison, becoming more and more desperate. On 7 May, he had written a final letter to Dzerzhinsky, reminding him of his promise of release in exchange for a complete confession. He asked either to be shot, or to be given work, as he could not bear to linger in jail. That evening, after a drive to Jaroslavl, where so many of his close colleagues had met their death, he flung himself – or was flung out – from a window of the prison. He crashed to his death in the prison courtyard. Five days later, the Soviet press announced the news of his 'suicide', and printed his last letter. Churchill has left this obituary of Savinkov. 'Whether he was quietly shot in prison, or committed suicide in his despair, is uncertain and unimportant. They had destroyed him body and soul. They had reduced his life's effort to meaningless grimace, had made him insult his cause, and had fouled his memory for ever. Yet when all is said and done, and with all the stains and tarnishes there be, few men tried more, gave more, dared more and suffered more for the Russian people.'

On 3 September, Reilly finally returned to Paris, where he was met by Boyce. After lengthy discussions with him, General Kutepov and others, it was agreed that Reilly should go to Helsinki to interview Marie Schultz and her husband. But on no account would he be lured back into Russia. He reached Helsinki on 21 September and there saw Marie Schultz, who told him that Reilly's and Savinkov's old networks had joined forces, and made contacts in high opposition circles. Next day, he wrote to Pepita in Paris that he was impressed with Marie Schultz. 'If only 25% of what she said is based on facts (and not on self-induced delusion, as is so often the case when the wish is the father of the will), then there is really something entirely new, powerful and worthwhile going on in Russia.'

But as yet there was no news from The Trust in the interior; a telegram was expected, and when it arrived, he would have to go to Viborg on the frontier for two days. He would have to take the boat back on 26 September, which would bring him to Stettin on 28 September. He wrote to Pepita a second time on 22 September: 'Just a few lines to tell you that the telegram has come, and that I am leaving tomorrow morning for Viborg. I shall write you whether I shall go from Stettin to Hamburg or to Berlin.'

On 24 September, Reilly duly went to Viborg, where he met Yakushev, whom he was satisfied was not an agent-provocateur, and who convinced him that The Trust was indeed a powerful underground movement. Yakushev urged him to go to Moscow for two days to meet the 'Shadow Government'. Most of The Trust leaders held such senior positions in Russia that their absence abroad would be noticed. Reilly agreed to leave the next day for Moscow.

On 25 September he wrote a letter to Pepita, which Bunakov was only to give her if he failed to return. 'It is absolutely necessary that I should go for three days to Petrograd and Moscow. I am leaving tonight, and will be back here on Tuesday morning (the 29th). I want you to know that I would not have undertaken this trip unless it was absolutely essential, and if I was not convinced that there is *practically* no risk attached to it.' He was only writing in the improbable case of a mishap. 'Should this happen, then you must not take *any* steps. They will help little, but may finally lead to giving the alarm to the Bolshies and to disclosing my identity.' If he was arrested, it could only be on some insignificant charge, and his 'new friends' were powerful enough to obtain his prompt release. 'I cannot imagine any circumstances under which the Bolshies could tumble to my identity – provided *nothing* is done from your side . . . Naturally, none of these people must get an inkling where I am and

137

what has happened to me . . .' That night, Reilly crossed from Finland into Russia, with a false passport in the name of Sternberg.

It is now established that it was never The Trust's original plan to kill, or even arrest Reilly. This would have defeated its own aims of quietly infiltrating and deluding its opponents. He was to be allowed to leave Russia safely. At first, all went well. Reilly reached Leningrad safely, and was met by Yakushev and a man in OGPU counter-intelligence. He spent the night in a comfortable flat, in the centre of the city. Next morning, he was driven to a villa in Malakhovka, just outside Moscow. The welcoming party, meanwhile, went to a flat in Moscow, while the man in OGPU counter-intelligence went to report the success of the first part of their mission. He was gone some time. The Trust representatives became uneasy; the OGPU had said that Reilly would indeed be allowed to leave Russia again; were they now going back on their word? Eventually, the man from OGPU returned; and they all went back to the villa. On the way, he pulled out a wad of money and instructed The Trust to purchase tickets for Reilly to leave by train for Leningrad and be back in Finland within two days, as originally planned.

On arrival at the villa, they found it surrounded by the secret police. Inside, things were strained. The conversation, as planned, never really got going. While Reilly waited in the sitting-room, a heated conversation took place in the hall between the OGPU and The Trust, who argued that if Reilly was not allowed to leave, then the whole Trust would break down, and lose all credibility. Finally, the OGPU admitted that cars were coming to take Reilly away. The Trust pleaded that they all go back to Moscow and discuss things. This was agreed. But on the way to the station, a pair of handcuffs was slipped over Reilly's wrists, and he was driven straight to the Lubyanka prison. The Soviet press then put out this statement: 'On the night of 28/29 September, four smugglers attempted to cross the Finnish frontier. Two

138

were killed, one, a Finnish soldier, taken prisoner and the fourth, mortally wounded, died on the way to Leningrad.'

It was later discovered that Reilly had been arrested on the orders of the Politbureau – especially those of Stalin.

At first Reilly was well treated by his captors. He was given Savinkov's well-furnished apartment and was even allowed to go for drives in the country, as Savinkov had been permitted. But when he refused to say anything at all, the OGPU got tough. He probably was not tortured himself, but simply made to witness some horrific torture and execution scenes. Finally, he cooperated. In an attempt to barter for his life, he gave the OGPU some details of the British Secret Service, and the Foreign Office. He was then of no further use. But they seem to have shown some indulgence in the way they disposed of their chief opponent. One morning, while Reilly was taking a walk in the Lenin Hills, he was shot in the back by a man named Ibrahim, the OGPU's crack marksman.

As the Soviet news agencies made no mention of Reilly's capture, there was great apprehension in official circles in London about what he might have told his captors. There was a complete clampdown in SIS circles. Boyce and other British agents who had been involved with Reilly were removed from their jobs. To try and provoke some action, Pepita had his death announced in *The Times*, but even this brought no response. Neither the SIS nor the Foreign Office would tell her anything.

Misgivings about The Trust grew considerably. By 1927, there were moves by the OGPU to liquidate their own creation. Various Trust employees defected. Finally, in June 1927, by which time England had broken off diplomatic relations with Soviet Russia, the assassination of the Soviet Ambassador in Warsaw coincided with a bomb attack in Leningrad. The Soviet news agency blamed both attacks on the British Government, and included other accusations of terrorism. It then made its first mention of the capture of Reilly, when it

139

stated: 'In the summer of 1925, a certain merchant carrying a Soviet passport with the name of Sternberg was wounded and arrested by the frontier guard, while illegally crossing the Finnish frontier. During the inquiry, a witness declared that his name was actually Sidney George Reilly, and that he was an English spy, a captain of the Royal Air Force, one of the chief organisers of "Lockhart's plot", who by sentence of the Tribunal of 3 December 1918, had been declared outlawed. Reilly declared that he came to Russia for the special purpose of organising terrorist acts, arson and revolts, and that when coming from America, he had seen Mr Churchill, Chancellor of the Exchequer, who personally instructed him as to the reorganisation of terrorist and other acts, calculated to create a diversion. His written testimony is in the possession of the (Soviet) Government. Reilly's evidence was entirely corroborated by material seized during further arrests.' Next day, a further communiqué contained a detailed confession which Reilly had allegedly made. But nothing was said of his fate.

Much of this statement is clearly untrue; but it was the first mention of Reilly's capture – and the absence of any news about his fate caused more misgiving. A question was asked in Parliament, and Pepita wrote to Churchill, but no more information was forthcoming.

A further question was asked in Parliament in 1931; but the Foreign Office spokesman could only reply: 'Inquiries were made early in 1929, through the Norwegian Legation in Moscow, and the Soviet authorities replied that Captain Reilly had been shot while attempting illegally to cross the frontier in September 1925. It does not, therefore, appear that further inquiries would yield any useful results.'

Finally, when Kruschev and Bulganin visited England in 1956, Sir Anthony Eden asked if they had any news of the fate of Reilly. There was no response to this request.

There is, in fact, no satisfactory account of what Reilly did tell Soviet intelligence. Perhaps the least unsatisfactory story is provided by a certain Captain van Narvig. It creates a link of sorts between Reilly and Philby, Burgess and Maclean. Van Narvig was a former officer of the Russian Imperial Army. But he was not really a Russian. In fact, he was one of that cosmopolitan band from whom secret agents are so easily recruited. Though born in St Petersburg of an English mother and a German father, he himself was actually a citizen of Finland. He was in Finland, having served on General Mannerheim's staff, in 1925, when Reilly passed through for the last time. Captain van Narvig has spoken at length with the author, Richard Deacon, and it is clear that he knew Reilly as well as it was possible to know him. In fact, he admits that he 'owed a lot to Sidney Reilly,' for general advice.

In Finland in 1925, van Narvig was convinced that The Trust was simply a branch of Soviet intelligence. 'There is no question at all that Reilly did not know he was entering a wolves' lair,' van Narvig told Richard Deacon. 'He was fully aware that The Trust was a cover for Russian counter-espionage agents.' But Reilly was 'romantically eager to re-organise Bolshevism, if he could not defeat it.'

Captain van Narvig was also partly responsible for the defection in 1937 of General Walter Krivitsky (head of Soviet Military Intelligence in Western Europe), who posed as an art dealer in Amsterdam as a cover. After his defection, Krivitsky sought refuge in the United States. But as a result of his dire warnings of the extent to which Soviet Russia had penetrated certain Western Intelligence services, it was arranged, early in the war, for Krivitsky to make a secret visit to England, and he provided enough evidence to convict of espionage a code clerk at the Foreign Office.

Krivitsky then returned to the United States, where he was given an American passport. But in London, there was a feeling that Krivitsky had been unusually reticent and knew more than he was prepared to say. 'He told me when he got back to New York,' states van Narvig, 'that he was certain he had made a great error in going to London. I asked him why, and he replied: "One just cannot trust the British. The Soviet Union have spies there in very high places. One never knows who is a friend or an enemy".'

Van Narvig became convinced that Krivitsky knew how and by whom British Intelligence had been penetrated by the Russians. He spoke of a recruiting agent 'in academic circles at Cambridge,' who found suitable candidates for Russian espionage. Krivitsky certainly knew all about Philby, for Philby met his first wife while on assignment for Soviet Intelligence in Vienna. Krivitsky also met his wife in Vienna – and the two girls were in the same underground communist cell. Moreover, Krivitsky made reference to the presence of a 'second traitor' in the Foreign Office, whose name was Scottish and whose habits were bohemian. The description neatly fits the traitor Donald Maclean.

Eventually, van Narvig told Krivitsky that he might be exaggerating things about the British. Krivitsky retorted: 'You know the agent Reilly. It was his information which enabled us to penetrate the British network. He thought by telling us a little, he could help Britain and save himself. In the end, he did not help Britain, and he did not save himself.'

Early in 1941, it was suggested that Krivitsky should pay a second visit to England. Within a few days of receiving that invitation, he was found dead in his hotel room, with the back of his head blown off.

Someone in London had evidently sent an urgent warning to Moscow that Krivitsky should not be allowed to return to England. A liquidation squad sent by the NKVD to the United States had been immediately alerted – and it was to be several more decades before all the traitors in the Foreign Office, and elsewhere in London, were exposed.

THE END

Sources

War Cabinet papers.
War Office papers: W.O,/0149 series.
Foreign Office papers: F.O./371 series.
Admiralty papers: Adm/137 series.

Bailey, Geoffrey. *The Conspirators* (London, 1961)
Bunyan, James. *Intervention, Civil War and Commun-
ism in Russia* (Baltimore, 1936)
Chester, Lewis et al. *The Zinoviev Letter* (London,
1967)
Churchill, Winston S. *Great Contemporaries* (London,
1965)
Deacon, Richard. *A History of the British Secret Service*
(London, 1969)
Degras, Jane. *Soviet Documents on Foreign Policy*
(London, 1951)
Freund, Gerald. *Unholy Alliance* (London, 1957)
Hansard
Harvard Library Bulletin (1970)
Hill, George. *Go Spy the Land* (London, 1932)
Jones, Thomas. *Whitehall Dairy*, vol 1 (London, 1969)
Kennan, George. *Russia and the West under Lenin and
Stalin* (London, 1961)
Kettle, Michael. *The Allies and the Russian Collapse*
(London, 1981)
Latsis, M. Y. *Two Years of Struggle on the Internal Front*
(Moscow, 1920)
Lloyd George papers. F203/3/6; F10/1/53; F10/2/60
Lockhart, Robert Bruce. *Memoirs of a British Agent*
(London, 1932)

Marchand, Réné. *Allied Agents in Soviet Russia* (London, 1918)

Oudendyk, W. J. *Ways and Byways in Diplomacy* (London, 1931)

Reilly, Sidney. *The Adventures of Sidney Reilly* (London, 1931)

Riezler, Kurt. *Diaries, Essays, Documents* (Gottingen, 1972)

Trotsky Papers, vol 1. 1917–1919 (The Hague, 1964)

Ullman, Richard. *Intervention and the War* (London, 1961)

Young, Kenneth. *The Diaries of Sir Robert Bruce Lockhart, 1915–1918* (London, 1973)

The Times
Morning Post
Pravda
Izvestia